AP® HUMAN GEOGRAPHY
CRASH COURSE®

By Dr. Christian Sawyer

D0047993

 Research & Education Association
Visit our website at: www.rea.com

Research & Education Association
61 Ethel Road West
Piscataway, New Jersey 08854
E-mail: info@rea.com

AP® HUMAN GEOGRAPHY CRASH COURSE®

Published 2015

Copyright © 2012 by Research & Education Association, Inc.
All rights reserved. No part of this book may be reproduced
in any form without permission of the publisher.

Printed in the United States of America

Library of Congress Control Number 2011929570

ISBN-13: 978-0-7386-0932-4
ISBN-10: 0-7386-0932-3

AP HUMAN GEOGRAPHY CRASH COURSE TABLE OF CONTENTS

PART I

INTRODUCTION

PART II

KEY CONTENT REVIEW

Test-Taking Strategies

ABOUT THIS BOOK

REA's *AP Human Geography Crash Course* is the first book of its kind for the last-minute studier or any AP student who wants a quick refresher on the course. The *Crash Course* is based on a careful analysis of the AP Human Geography Course Description outline and actual AP test questions.

Written by an AP teacher, our easy-to-read format gives students a crash course in Human Geography. The targeted review chapters are grouped by topics, offering you a concise way to learn all the important ideas, facts, and terms before exam day.

Unlike other test preps, REA's *AP Human Geography Crash Course* gives you a review specifically focused on what you really need to study in order to ace the exam. The introduction discusses the keys for success and shows you strategies to help you build your overall point score.

Part Two is a complete crash course in Human Geography. These 10 chapters focus on the subjects tested on the AP exam and cover everything from the Nature and Perspectives of Geography to Cities and Urban Land Use.

Part Three focuses exclusively on test-taking tactics for the AP Human Geography exam. The author provides expert advice on how to master both the multiple-choice and free-response sections. Each chapter gives you specific strategies for success that will help you raise your overall point score.

No matter how or when you prepare for the AP Human Geography exam, REA's Crash Course will show you how to study efficiently and strategically, so you can boost your score!

To check your test readiness for the AP Human Geography exam, either before or after studying this *Crash Course*, take REA's **FREE online practice exam**. To access your practice exam, visit the online REA Study Center at *www.rea.com/studycenter* and follow the on-screen instructions. This true-to-format test features automatic scoring, detailed explanations of all answers, and will help you identify your strengths and weaknesses so you'll be ready on exam day!

Good luck on your AP Human Geography exam!

ABOUT OUR AUTHOR

 **Christian Sawyer**, Ed.D., is a nationally-recognized Social Studies teacher who has implemented and taught AP Human Geography and other social studies courses at both the high school and college levels for nearly a decade. In addition to his high school teaching in Kentucky and Tennessee, Dr. Sawyer currently serves as Assistant Principal for Academics at St. Thomas More High School in Lafayette, Louisiana, where he is leading academic initiatives including a 21st-century learning technologies transfomation. Previously, he served as the "Teacher in Residence" at Vanderbilt University's top-ranked Peabody College of Education, where he taught courses in Human Geography and Social Studies Education. Additionally, he has been a guest instructor in Taiwan, an instructor of Geopolitics at the Johns Hopkins Center for Talented Youth, and an Atlantik-Brueke Fellow studying post-War German-American relations and East/West German integration.

Dr. Sawyer's work in advocating for broader geographic awareness led to his recognition as a 2006 National Outstanding Social Studies Teacher of the Year by the National Council for the Social Studies; the 2006 Tennessee Outstanding Social Studies Teacher of the Year by the Tennessee Council for the Social Studies; a White House Fellows Regional Finalist; a 2008 Tennessee Distinguished Educator; the recipient of the "2008 Educator Award" from the Nashville Mayor's Commission on People with Disabilities; and a "Local Hero" by Vanderbilt University. Dr. Sawyer has written and edited English and Social Studies curriculum for the Modern Red Schoolhouse Institute and other publishers, including his test preparation book on AP Human Geography, published by Research & Education Association.

Dr. Sawyer has also chaired a host of state and national Social Studies committees. He is a leading voice in chartering curricular integration for the Tennessee Department of Education's Commission for Targeting Cross-Curricular Integration. A native of Louisville, Kentucky, Dr. Sawyer graduated with highest distinction, Phi Beta Kappa, from the Honors Program at the University of North Carolina at Chapel Hill. After earning his master's degree and being inducted into the nation's oldest education honor society, Kappa Delta Pi, Dr. Sawyer earned his doctorate at Vanderbilt University.

ACKNOWLEDGMENTS

In addition to our author, we would like to thank Larry B. Kling, Vice President, Editorial, for his overall guidance, which brought this publication to completion; Pam Weston, Publisher, for setting the quality standards for production and managing the publication to completion; Diane Goldschmidt, Senior Editor, for editorial project management; Alice Leonard, Senior Editor, for preflight editorial review; and Weymouth Design, for designing our cover.

We would also like to extend special thanks to Benjamin Shultz of the University of Tennessee-Knoxville for technically reviewing the manuscript, Marianne L'Abbate for copyediting, and Kathy Caratozzolo of Caragraphics for typesetting this edition.

PART I
INTRODUCTION

Seven Keys to Success
on the AP Human Geography Exam

AP Human Geography is definitely one of the most empowering courses you can take in high school. So many students walk out of their AP Human Geo experience feeling as if they learned more about the world—and themselves—than they ever expected. However, for many students, preparing for the AP exam can seem like a steep mountain to climb and can feel overwhelming. But it doesn't have to overwhelm you—preparing for the AP Human Geography exam can be greatly improved by studying strategically and efficiently. In order to succeed on the exam, you should focus your preparation by gaining an understanding of the structure of the AP Human Geography exam itself and reviewing the key topics that are tested.

This *Crash Course* book contains the essential information for you to target in your preparation for the exam. This book is written specifically to help you focus your preparation for exam success—containing key topics and concepts you need to know in order to score well on the exam. This book is designed with you, the student, in mind. It will show you what you already know and how to succeed on the AP Human Geography exam.

Specifically, this first chapter gives you an overview of keys to success on the exam and analysis of key patterns and data from previous exams that will help you study more strategically. Chapters 2 through 12 provide you with a targeted review of the AP Human Geography topics assessed on the exam—key models, terms, concepts, and facts. The final chapters review strategies for success on the AP exam questions, offering you tools for navigating both the multiple-choice and free-response sections of the AP Human Geography exam. Also, you will find "test tips" to enrich your exam preparations throughout this book. Remember: Succeeding on the AP Human Geography exam is definitely within your reach, especially if you study strategically with this *Crash Course* book!

KEY 1: Understanding the Structure of the AP Human Geography Exam

1. The AP Human Geography exam is given each May and is approximately two hours and 15 minutes long.

2. The exam is divided into two sections: a 60-minute multiple-choice section and a 75-minute free-response section.

Test Section	Task	Time	Percent of Exam Score
Multiple Choice	About 75 questions	60 minutes	50%
Short Break		10–15 minutes	
Free Response	3 free-response questions	75 minutes	50%

3. Each section of the exam is completed separately, and each counts for half of the student's score.

4. The College Board, which creates and administers the AP Human Geography exam, creates a formula (which changes slightly every year) to convert a student's exam performance into an AP Human Geography exam score ranging from 1 (lowest) to 5 (highest). In general, an exam score of 3, 4, or 5 is considered "passing" and compares roughly to the following grades in an introductory Human Geography course in college:

AP Human Geography Exam Score	Grade in a College Human Geography Course
5	A
4	B
3	C
2	D

5. Some colleges and universities accept scores of 3, 4, or 5 for college credit, but some only accept 4s and 5s. Some colleges do not award credit for the AP test, so it is important for you to research a college's policy. Remember, however, that even if a college does not award credit for an AP test, it usually still strengthens your college application to have risen to the "AP challenge."

KEY 2: Understanding How the AP Human Geography Exam Is Scored

1. The exact formula that will be used to calculate your exam score varies from year to year. The College Board has, however, released its scoring formula for the 2006 AP Human Geography exam (the most recently released AP Human Geography exam).

2. The score-setting equation for the 2006 Released AP Human Geography exam was:

Section I—Multiple-Choice Raw Score:

$$\underline{\hspace{3cm}} \; 0.8108 = \underline{\hspace{3cm}}$$

Number
multiple-choice
questions correct
(out of 74)

Weighted
Section I Score

Section II—Free-Response Section Raw Score:

FRQ 1 Score $\underline{\hspace{2cm}}$ × 2.2222 = $\underline{\hspace{2cm}}$
(out of 9)   A

FRQ 2 Score $\underline{\hspace{2cm}}$ × 2.5000 = $\underline{\hspace{2cm}}$
(out of 8)   B

FRQ 3 Score $\underline{\hspace{2cm}}$ × 3.33 = $\underline{\hspace{2cm}}$
(out of 6)   C

A + B + C = Weighted Section II Score

Test Tip

Be aware that the order in which the free-response questions are presented has little to do with the level of difficulty or the topic. Each FRQ is equally important, and each counts as a significant portion of your exam grade.

2006 Composite Score Calculation and Conversion Table:

Weighted Section I Score + Weighted Section II Score = Composite Score

2006 AP Human Geography Composite Score Range	2006 AP Exam Grade
74–120	5
59–73	4
45–58	3
35–44	2
0–34	1

Notice that for the 2006 exam, a student only needed about 1/3 the total possible points to earn a score of a 3. To earn a 4, you only needed about half the total possible points on the AP exam (59/120). This is very good news! You only need to earn *half* the total possible points to earn a 4 and get college credit!

KEY 3: Understanding the Distribution of Previous Exam Scores

	Approximate % of Students Earning AP Human Geography Exam Score of				
Year	5	4	3	2	1
2013	12	20	21	19	28
2012	13	20	20	18	30
2011	12	18	21	18	32

(Data obtained from College Board Student Grade Distribution Reports)

1. Analysis of score distributions from 2011-2013 indicates that about 1 in 2 test takers (50 percent) earned a 3, 4, or 5 on the AP Human Geography exam.

2. About 1 in 8 students (12 percent) earned the highest score of a 5, whereas about 1 in 3 earned the lowest score of a 1.

3. The number of AP Human Geography test-takers has been increasing each year, as the course is gaining popularity across the nation.

KEY 4: Understanding the Multiple-Choice Section of the Exam

1. The multiple-choice section of the exam has approximately 75 questions, each with five possible answer choices.

2. Each multiple-choice question counts equally towards a student's score, and points are not deducted for an incorrect answer. This means that it is in your best interest to answer *every* multiple-choice question on the exam.

3. Many students think that AP exams ask multiple-choice questions that are random, but the test writers of the AP Human Geography exam actually follow a pattern. Here is an approximate breakdown of the topics covered in the multiple-choice questions on the exam:

AP Human Geography Topic	Approximate percentage of MC questions on the exam
Geography: Its Nature and Perspectives	5–10%
Population (and Migration)	13–17%
Cultural Patterns and Processes	13–17%
Political Organization of Space	13–17%
Agriculture, Food Production, and Rural Land Use	13–17%
Industrialization and Economic Development	13–17%
Cities and Urban Land Use	13–17%

4. Analysis of the 2006 Released AP Human Geography exam provides insight into how many questions you should aim to answer correctly in order to pass:

Range of Multiple-Choice Questions Correct on 2006 exam (out of 74)	2006 AP Human Geography Exam Scores
53–60	Most of these test-takers scored a 5
45–52	Most of these test-takers scored 4s and 5s
36–44	Most of these test-takers scored 3s and 4s
28–35	Most of these test-takers scored 2s and 3s
19–27	Most of these test-takers scored 1s and 2s
0–18	Most of these test-takers scored a 1

(Source: Released test data for 2006 AP Human Geography exam from the College Board)

- Nearly 99% of the 2006 test-takers who answered between 53 and 60 of the 74 multiple-choice questions correctly scored a 5 on the AP Human Geography exam.

- Nearly 50% of the test-takers who got 36 to 44 of the multiple-choice questions correct scored a 4 on the exam.

- Most of the test-takers who got between 28-44 multiple-choice questions correct out of the 74 questions (about half of the multiple-choice questions) scored a 3.

- **Remember** that your AP test score will depend on your performance on the multiple-choice section *and* on the free-response section. The weighted scores are combined to give you your overall exam score.

KEY 5: Understanding the Free-Response Section of the Exam

1. After completing the multiple-choice section of the exam, students will be given a short 10- to 15-minute break. Once the break ends, the free-response section begins.

2. In the free-response section, students are asked to answer three constructed-response questions in the allotted 75 minutes.

3. Often, free-response questions (called FRQs) ask students to respond to or analyze a graph, photo, diagram, etc.

4. Students are expected to use their analytical and organizational skills in writing their responses.

5. While writing a formal essay is not required, simply listing facts is not likely to receive a high score.

Test Tip

AP readers (educators who score the FRQs) advise that a key strategy for doing well on the FRQ section of the exam is to keep focused, be succinct, and don't distract the reader with extraneous, non-related information. Make sure everything you write down is directly in response to the question.

6. All three FRQs are required to be answered. Leaving an FRQ blank or writing a completely unrelated response to an FRQ has a very negative impact on your chances of earning a 3, 4, or 5 on the exam.

7. The AP readers use a "points awarded" system, which means that they only give points for correct elements in your responses—they do not take points away. The AP Readers look for key words and phrases in your answer that are tied to the rubrics they use to score the FRQs. When they see those key words and phrases, they mark a point for you and move on.

KEY 6: Understanding Previous AP Exam FRQ topics, 2002–2014

Year	Topics tested in FRQ 1	Topics tested in FRQ 2	Topics tested in FRQ 3
2002	Nation, state, nation-state	Religion and cultural landscape	Gender and space
2003	Core-periphery model and development, central place theory	Tourism and regional landscape distinctiveness, time-space compression	Demographic transition model and international migration in Europe
2004	Maquiladoras, international division of labor, core-periphery	Rural space, agribusiness, U.S. poultry	Bid-rent, population pyramids, North American urban space (central business district)
2005	Supranationalism/ devolution	U.S. migration streams and push/pull factors	Gentrification, North American urban space
2006	International migration streams, core-periphery, distance decay, chain migration	Footloose industry, outsourcing, de-industrialization, U.S. tertiary-transition	Centripetal/ Centrifugal forces
2007	Von Thünen model	Lingua franca, language diffusion	New international division of labor
2008	Von Thünen model vs. Burgess Concentric Zone Model	U.S. migration streams (net in, net out migration)	Education, gender gap, human development index, and development in the periphery

Year	Topics tested in FRQ 1	Topics tested in FRQ 2	Topics tested in FRQ 3
2009	Map reading skills, folk/ethnic religions	Urban space and development in global periphery (squatter settlements)	Agribusiness in U.S. (dairy farming vs. organic farming)
2010	Weber theory of industrial location	National identity and economic, political (forward capital) centripetal and ethnic and infrastructural centrifugal forces	Demographic transition model and economic development
2011	Urban geography—private city vs. rank-size rule	Thomas Malthus's theory on population growth	Industrial location models
2012	Influence of boundaries and walls on cultural landscape	Subsistence agriculture, shifting cultivation	Distributions of religion and impact on cultural landscape
2013	High tech corridors, agglomeration	Demography and graying populations	Urbanization and transportation
2014	Rostow's five-stage model of economic growth vs. Wallerstein's world system theory	Types of boundaries and relationship to colonialism in Africa	Agricultural systems

This table provides some important insights into FRQs:

1. The FRQ questions often probe your knowledge from different topics in the AP Human Geography curriculum.

2. Both geographic models and key concepts are often tested in the questions.

3. Even if the topics were tested on an FRQ in a prior year, they are still fair game—notice that in 2007 and in 2008, an FRQ related to the von Thünen model.

4. The FRQs have never yet asked students to write from memory every piece of a geographic model, but they often ask you to use a particular geographic model in analyzing an issue or pattern. Applying the lessons of the geographic model is a vital skill.

5. While an FRQ question addresses, for example, Weber and industrial location, it is not a good idea to prepare by simply memorizing what Weber said. The question will probably ask you to apply your knowledge of Weber and industrial location and how those principles influence the industrial landscape.

KEY 7: Using College Board and REA Materials to Supplement Your Crash Course

1. Your Crash Course contains *essential* information for the AP Human Geography exam. You should, however, supplement this book with materials from your course and the College Board.

2. The AP Human Geography Course Description Booklet and the 2001 and 2006 AP Human Geography Released Exams can be ordered from the College Board's online store.

3. Additionally, the College Board's AP Central website contains outstanding review materials, including all of the free-response questions ever asked on the past AP Human Geography exams and practice multiple-choice questions.

4. Also, REA's *AP Human Geography All Access*™ Book + Web + Mobile study system further enhances your exam preparation by offering a comprehensive review book plus a suite of online assessments (topic-level quizzes, mini-tests, a full-length practice test, and e-flashcards), all designed to pinpoint your strengths and weaknesses and help focus your study for the exam.

Key Geographic
Models and Theories

1. Demographic Transition Model (DTM)

   In the four stages of transition from an agricultural
   subsistence economy to an industrialized country,
   demographic patterns move from extremely high birth and
   death rates to low birth and death rates. In the process,
   population growth rates skyrocket and then fall again. The
   crude death rate first falls because of the influx of better
   health technology, and then the birth rate gradually falls to
   match the new social structure.

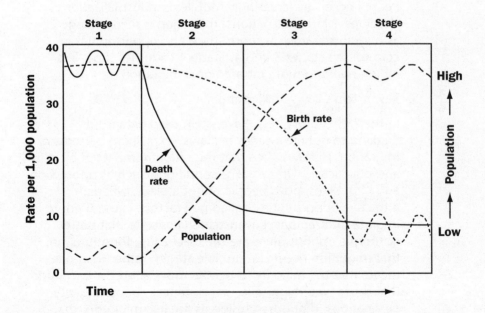

Demographic Transition Model

2. Epidemiologic Transition Model

   Disease vulnerability shifts in patterns similar to the DTM. In the early stages, plague and pestilence spread as a result of poor medical technology. As industrialization proceeds, diseases related to urban life spread. In later stages, diseases once thought eradicated reappear as more-developed societies come into easier contact with less-developed regions struggling with the more primitive diseases, such as smallpox and the bubonic plague. Leading causes of death in later stages are related to diseases associated with aging, such as heart disease.

3. Gravity Model of Spatial Interaction

   When applied to migration, larger places attract more migrants than do smaller places. Additionally, destinations that are more distant have a weaker pull effect than do closer opportunities of the same caliber.

4. Zelinsky Model of Migration Transition

   Migration trends follow demographic transition stages. People become increasingly mobile as industrialization develops. More international migration is seen in stage 2 as migrants search for more space and opportunities in countries in stages 3 and 4. Stage 4 countries show less emigration and more intraregional migration.

5. Ravenstein's Laws of Migration

   In the 19th century, E.G. Ravenstein used data from England to outline a series of "laws" explaining patterns of migration. His laws state that migration is impacted by push and pull factors. Unfavorable conditions, such as oppression and high taxes, push people out of a place, whereas attractive opportunities, called pull factors, cause them to migrate into regions. Ravenstein's laws state that better economic opportunities are the chief cause for migration; that migration occurs in multiple stages, rather than one move; that the majority of people move short distances and that those who migrate longer distances choose big-city destinations; that urban residents are less migratory than rural residents; that for every migration stream, there is a counterstream; and factors such as gender, age, and socioeconomic level influence a person's likelihood to migrate. Keep in mind that his "laws" applied to the timeframe and context of his analysis.

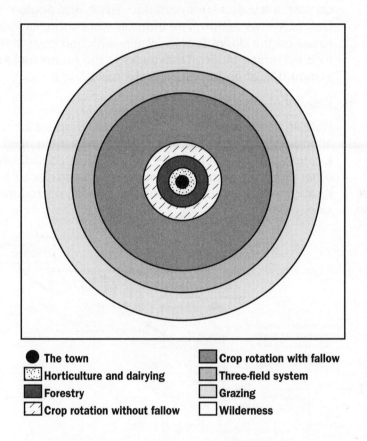

● The town
▒ Horticulture and dairying
■ Forestry
▨ Crop rotation without fallow

■ Crop rotation with fallow
■ Three-field system
☐ Grazing
☐ Wilderness

Von Thünen's Model of Agricultural Land Use

6. Von Thünen Model

   Developed by German geographer Johann Heinrich von Thünen, this model explains and predicts agricultural land use patterns in a theoretical state by varying transportation cost. Given the model's assumptions, the pattern that emerges predicts more-intensive rural land uses closer to the marketplace, and more-extensive rural land uses farther from the city's marketplace. These rural land use zones are divided in the model into concentric rings.

7. Least Cost Theory

   This is Alfred Weber's theory of industrial location, explaining and predicting where industries will locate based on cost analysis of transportation, labor, and agglomeration factors. Weber assumes an industry will choose its location based on the desire to minimize production costs and thus maximize profits. Drawbacks to the model include its assumption of an immobile and equal labor force.

8. Locational Interdependence

   Hotelling's theory of locational interdependence asserts that an industry's locational choices are heavily influenced by the location of their chief competitors and related industries. In other words, industries do not make isolated decisions on locations without considering where other, related industries exist.

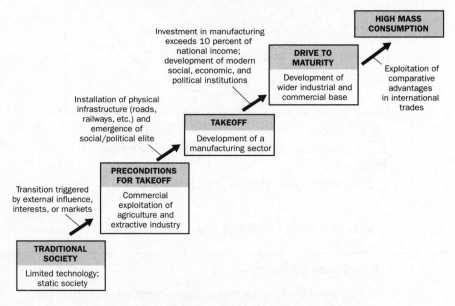

Rostow's Stages of Economic Development

9. Rostow's Modernization Model

   Developed in the 1950s, this model exemplifies the liberal development ideology, as opposed to structuralist theory.

Under this model, all countries develop in a five-stage process. The development cycle is initiated by investment in a takeoff industry that allows the country to grow a comparative advantage, which sparks greater economic gain that eventually diffuses throughout the country's economy. Drawbacks to this model include its not identifying cultural and historic differences in development trajectories because it is based on North American and western European development histories.

10. Borchert's Model of Urban Evolution

   Borchert created this model in the 1960s to predict and explain the growth of cities in four phases of transportation history: stage 1, the "sail wagon" era of 1790–1830; stage 2, the "iron horse" era of 1830–1870; stage 3, the "steel rail" epoch of 1870–1920; and stage 4, the current era of car and air travel that began after 1920.

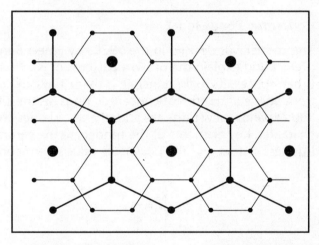

- • Village
- ⬤ Low-Order Central Place
- ⬤ High-Order Central Place
- —— Low-Order Market Area Boundary
- —— High-Order Market Area Boundary

Hexagonal Market Areas Predicted by Christaller's Central Place Theory

11. Central Place Theory

   Developed in the 1930s by Walter Christaller, this model explains and predicts patterns of urban places across the map. In his model, Christaller analyzed the hexagonal, hierarchical pattern of cities, villages, towns, and hamlets arranged according to their varying degrees of centrality, determined by the central place functions existing in urban places and the hinterlands they serve.

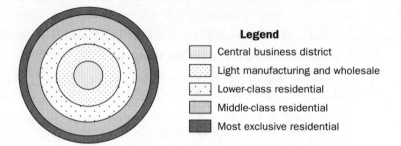

Legend

| Central business district
| Light manufacturing and wholesale
| Lower-class residential
| Middle-class residential
| Most exclusive residential

Concentric Zone Urban Land Use Model

12. Concentric Zone Model

This model was devised in the 1920s by Ernest Burgess to predict and explain the growth patterns of North American urban spaces. Its main principle is that cities can be viewed from above as a series of concentric rings; as the city grows and expands, new rings are added and old ones change character. Key elements of the model are the central business district and the peak land value intersection.

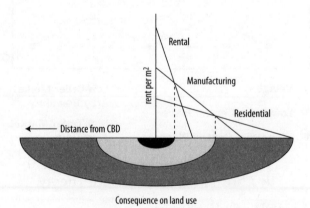

Bid-Rent Curve

13. Bid-Rent Curve

    Bid-rent curves show the variations in rent different users
    are willing to pay for land at different distances from some
    peak point of accessibility and visibility in the market, often
    the CBD. Because transportation costs increase as you
    move away from the market (often the CBD), rents usually
    decrease as distance increases from the market. Importantly,
    different types of land use (commercial retail, industrial,
    agriculture, housing) generate different bid-rent curves. Bid-
    rent curves explain the series of concentric rings of land use
    found in the concentric zone model.

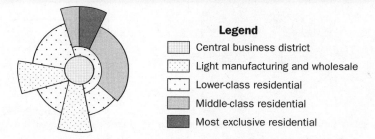

Legend

  Central business district

  Light manufacturing and wholesale

  Lower-class residential

  Middle-class residential

  Most exclusive residential

Sector Model of Urban Land Use

14. Sector Model

    This model, conceived by Homer Hoyt, predicts and explains
    North American urban growth patterns in the 1930s in a
    pattern in which similar land uses and socioeconomic groups
    clustered in linear sectors radiating outward from a central
    business district, usually along transportation corridors.

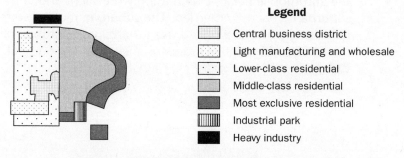

Legend

  Central business district

  Light manufacturing and wholesale

  Lower-class residential

  Middle-class residential

  Most exclusive residential

  Industrial park

  Heavy industry

Multiple-Nuclei Model of Urban Land Use

15. Multiple-Nuclei Model

Developed in the 1950s by Chauncy Harris and Edward Ullman, this model explains the changing growth pattern of urban spaces based on the assumption that growth occurred independently around several major foci (or nodes), many of which are far away from the central business district and only marginally connected to it.

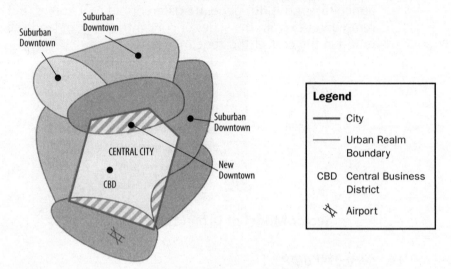

Urban Realms Model

16. Urban Realms Model

James Vance developed this model in the 1970s to explain and predict changing urban growth patterns as the automobile became increasingly prevalent and large suburban "realms" emerged. The suburban regions were functionally tied to a mixed-use suburban downtown, or mini-CBD, with relative independence from the original CBD.

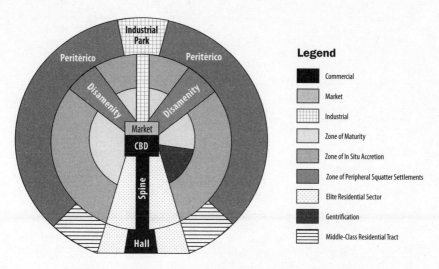

Latin American City Model (Griffin-Ford Model)

17. Latin American City Model

   Larry Ford and Ernest Griffin created a model of the pattern of urban growth in Latin America. Their model contains elements of Latin American culture and imprints of colonization and globalization, such as a prominent plaza and heavy growth around the CBD. However, in the Latin American pattern shown in their model, residential quality decreases with distance from the CBD. The model also presents a zone of maturity, populated with services and a wealthier population; a zone of squatter settlements, where recent urban migrants set up makeshift housing; and a zone of *in situ* accretion, which is a transitional zone that shows signs of transition to a zone of maturity.

Check out REA's **AP Human Geography** *test prep book for practice drills to quiz your memory of key terms and models in AP Human Geography. There are also many practice FRQs and multiple-choice questions, categorized by test theme and similar to questions you will face on the actual AP Human Geography exam. When using the practice-exam questions, be sure to read the explanations for each question. The explanations will help train your thinking and improve your performance on the exam.*

PART II

KEY CONTENT
Review

Geography:
Its Nature and Perspectives

I. **Geographers Have a Spatial Perspective**

A. Spatial Perspective

1. Geographers have a *spatial perspective* when they look at the world.

2. Geographers are most interested in looking into space (as in area, not "outer-space") and identifying, explaining, and predicting the human and physical patterns that develop across space over time as well as the interconnections among spaces and places.

   i. For example, a geographer might be interested in drawing a map of a state or a forest, or she might be interested in how the spatial pattern of a religion has changed over time.

B. The Five Themes

1. Location

   i. Location explains where something is on the Earth and the effects that position has on human life.

   ii. *Absolute location* is described by something's location on the global grid, the intersection of latitude and longitude.

   > ➤ *Lines of latitude (parallels)* are measured in degrees north or south of the equator, whereas *lines of longitude (meridians)* are measured in degrees east or west of the prime meridian.

> ➤ Only the equator can serve as the baseline for latitude because it is the only line of latitude that divides the Earth into two halves, or *hemispheres.*

> ➤ Technically, any line of longitude could serve as zero degrees longitude. The prime meridian, which runs through Greenwich, England, was selected when England was a prime naval power.

> ➤ *Greenwich Mean Time (GMT)* is based on the prime meridian.

   iii. *Relative location* is described by something's relationship to places around it.

> ➤ "Hillsboro High School is located 9 miles southwest of McGavock High School" is an example of describing the relative location of Hillsboro High School.

   iv. *Site and situation* also describe a place's location.

> ➤ *Site* refers to a place's internal physical and cultural characteristics, such as its terrain and dominant religions.

> ➤ *Situation* refers to the location (or context) of a place relative to the physical and cultural characteristics around it. The more interconnected a place is to other powerful places, the better its situation.

2. Human Environment Interaction

   i. Describes how human activities affect their environment and how environmental changes impact human life.

   ii. *Cultural ecology* is the study of the aspects and outcomes of human–environment interaction.

3. Regions

   i. A *region* is a spatial unit, or group of places, that share similar characteristics.

   ii. There are three types of regions:

➤ A *formal region* (or uniform region) is an area that has common cultural or physical features.

— The Sahara is a formal region, as is the area known as the "The Rockies."

— A map displaying where Islam is practiced is showing a formal region.

➤ A *functional region* (or nodal region) is a group of places linked together by some type of movement (or function).

— A map showing a group of places all infected by a type of disease would be showing a functional region.

— The *node* is the place in the functional region where the movement started.

➤ A *perceptual region* (or vernacular) is a group of places linked together because of perceptions about those places.

— For example, the region of the United States that is called "the South" is actually a perceptual region because the boundaries defining where "the South" exists are based on opinions. Think about how people disagree about whether Kentucky is part of the North or the South.

4. Place

   i. *Place* refers to all of the human and physical attributes in a location.

   ii. Human attributes of place include elements such as the religions, languages, political organizations, clothing, and artwork present in a location.

   iii. Physical attributes of place include climate, terrain, and natural resources in a location.

   iv. Often, the human and physical traits in a location give it a *"sense of place"* that is different from other places. Think of how your "sense" of your favorite place to read is different from your "sense" of your favorite movie theatre. Think of how the "sense of place" of Chicago differs from the "sense of place" of San Francisco.

5. Movement

    i.   Geographers analyze all of the types of *movement* in a space—movement of information, people, goods, and other phenomena.

    ii. Geographers also analyze how places interact with each other, a process known as *spatial interaction.*

    iii. In analyzing movement and spatial interaction, geographers often analyze *friction of distance,* or the degree to which distance interferes or reduces the amount of interaction between two places.

    iv. *Distance decay* occurs when the intensity of some phenomenon decreases as distance from it increases. For example, the intensity of sound decreases as you walk away from the stage of a rock concert.

    v. *Space-time compression* is the increasing sense that the world is "becoming smaller." Humans in distant places can feel closer together because of improved communication and transportation technologies, which reduce the friction of distance.

II. Geographic Models

A. Geographic Models

1. Geographers create *geographic models* to understand why spatial patterns exist in the ways they do and to predict how spatial patterns might change over time.

2. The Demographic Transition Model (DTM) is an example of a geographic model that helps explain and predict patterns in population change over time.

3. It is important to think about the history and region on which a geographic model is based and the drawbacks that exist when applying it to understand a different context.

i. For example, the DTM was based largely on British history. If you want to use the DTM to understand Chinese birth and death rates, you have to analyze the aspects of the DTM that apply to the Chinese situation as well as aspects of the DTM that are not a "good fit" for explaining and predicting Chinese patterns of population change.

➤ One difference involves the sheer size of the European population patterns on which the DTM was based, which were much smaller than China's current, far larger population size.

➤ The existence of restrictive population policies in China, such as the one-child policy, is another difference between Chinese demographic transition and the condition on which the DTM is based.

The AP exam often tests students' knowledge of geographic models and students' abilities to apply the models, rather than to just define them. So, don't just memorize what the models predict, but think about how the models can be applied. Also think about the shortcomings/limitations of applying the models under different conditions than those upon which the models were designed.

B. Physical Versus Human Geography

1. *Physical geography* is primarily concerned with spatial analysis of the Earth's natural phenomena, such as where and why patterns of climate, soil, and topography exist on the Earth.

2. *Human geography* is primarily concerned with spatial analysis of human patterns on the Earth and their interactions with the Earth—such as where and why patterns of religions, governments, languages, population, and economies exist on the Earth.

3. Both physical and human geography work to explain the patterns they see. In other words, they both seek to answer

the question *"WHY of WHERE."* But each approaches the question from different angles. Human geographers look primarily at patterns of human creation whereas physical geographers look primarily at naturally occurring patterns.

III. Mapmaking

A. Cartography

1. A *map* is a two-dimensional model of the Earth or a portion of it.

2. *Cartography* is the process of making a map.

   i.   All cartographers get rid of unnecessary details, a process called *simplification.*

B. Distortion

1. It is impossible to take the Earth's round surface and project it onto a flat surface without *distortion,* or error resulting from the "flattening" (or projection) process.

2. A *globe* is the most accurate representation of the Earth.

C. Four Properties of Maps

1. *Shape* refers to the geometric shapes of the objects on the map.

2. *Size* (area) refers to the relative amount of space taken up on the map by landforms or objects on a map.

3. *Distance* refers to the represented distance between objects on the map.

4. *Direction* refers to the degree of accuracy representing the *cardinal directions*—north, south, east, west—and their *intermediate directions*—northwest, northeast, southwest, and southeast.

D. Projections

1. *Cartographers* choose which properties of maps to distort by thinking about the map's purpose.

2. The Gall-Peters projection is *equal area* (or equivalent) because it accurately represents the actual area of landforms, but distorts other properties (like shape).

3. The Mercator projection (below) is *conformal* because it accurately represents the shape of landforms, but it is not equal in area because sizes of landforms are drastically distorted (Greenland, for example, is far larger on the map than it should be).

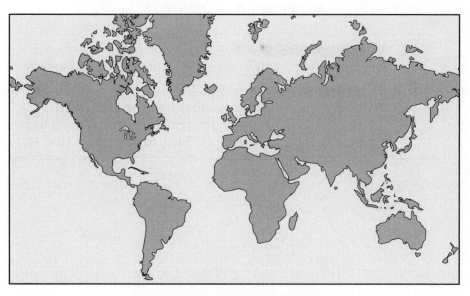

A Mercator Projection Map

4. *Equidistant* projections maintain distance, but distort other properties.

5. The Robinson projection is called a *compromise* projection because it is neither equal area nor conformal. Instead, all four properties are slightly distorted so that one property is not drastically distorted.

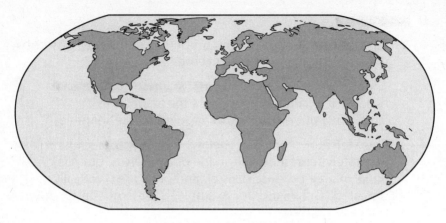

A Robinson Projection Map

6. *Azimuthal projections* are flat-plan constructed maps of each hemisphere; direction is accurate and great circles are evident.

   i. *Great circle routes* are formed on the surface of the Earth by passing a plane through the center of the Earth. The equator and every line of longitude paired with its twin on the opposite side of the Earth form great circles. Any arc of a great circle shows the shortest distance between two points on the Earth's surface.

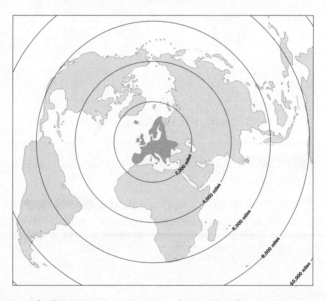

Azimuthal Projection Centered on Hamburg, Germany

E. Cognitive Maps

1. *Cognitive (or mental) maps* are drawn from memory and often reflect the spatial perceptions of those who draw them.

2. It is important to look not only at what is present on a cognitive map but also at what is left off a mental map.

F. Scale

1. *Map (or cartographic) scale* refers to the relationship between distance on the map and the actual measurement in the real world.

    i. The larger the area of space being represented on the map, the smaller its scale. A scale of 1:40 miles means 1 inch on the map equals 40 miles in the real world.

2. *Scale of inquiry* refers to the scope of a geographic analysis, such as whether the analysis is studying something affecting just a village or the entire world.

G. Categories of Maps

1. *Reference maps* show common features such as boundaries, roads, and mountains.

2. *Thematic maps* display one feature or pattern, such as climate, city size, or even number of alligators.

3. *Isoline thematic maps* display lines that connect points of equal value, such as elevation levels.

4. *Choropleth thematic maps* show patterns of some variable using colors or degrees of shading, such as population density.

5. *Proportional thematic maps* use symbols (a star, circle, triangle, etc.) to display the frequency of some variable. The larger the symbol on the map, the higher is the frequency of that variable found in that region.

6. *Dot density maps* are thematic maps that use equally-sized dots to represent the frequency of a variable in a given area.

7. A *cartogram* is a map that uses space on the map to show a particular variable.

   i.   For example, a cartogram showing the frequency of factory labor throughout the world would show a large space taken up by China and a smaller space taken up by the United States.

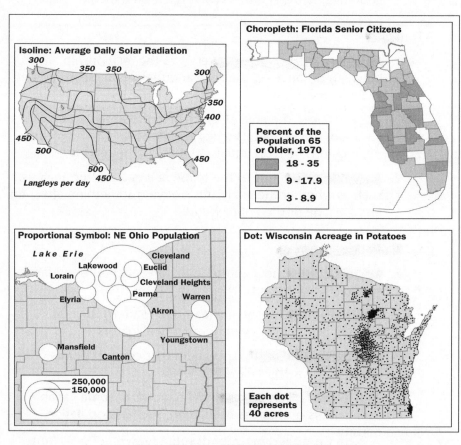

Four Types of Thematic Maps

Test Tip

The AP test has asked students to use different types of maps to find the answer to questions on the exam. As you study, be sure to flip through your textbook and look at different types of maps used in illustrations and to practice reading the maps to understand geographic patterns.

IV. Geographic Technology and Data

A. Geographic Information System (GIS)

  1. Refers to a computer program that stores geographic data and produces maps to show those data in space, often through layering data patterns over each other.

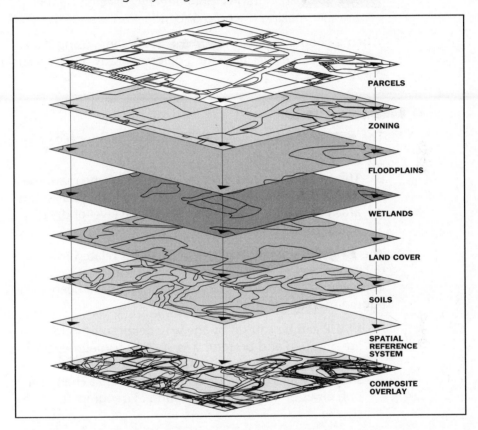

Layers of Data Compiled in a Geographic Information System

B. Remote Sensing

  1. Refers to the collection of information from satellites and distant collection systems not in physical contact with the objects being analyzed.

C. Global Position System (GPS)

   1. *GPS* uses satellite-driven remote sensing to determine exact locations on the global grid.

D. Primary Versus Secondary Data

   1. *Primary data* is geographic data directly collected by the geographer making the map or conducting the study.

   2. When a geographer uses *secondary data,* she is using data collected at an earlier time for a different study (e.g., census data).

E. Data Aggregation

   1. The *level of data aggregation* is the size of geographic units represented on a map.

      i. The larger the area being represented on the map, the *"coarser"* the level of data aggregation. The smaller the area being represented, the *"finer"* the level of data aggregation.

   2. The *modifiable areal unit problem (MAUP)* is related to data aggregation. MAUP is sometimes a source of error impacting spatial studies that use data that have been aggregated (or grouped).

      i. MAUP can be caused by the way geographic data are grouped and presented in studies: sometimes the boundaries used to group data in an areal unit are subjective and can be modified in ways that change outcomes or interpretations found in geographic studies.

         ➤ The boundaries used to group census data, such as those used to create census tracts, can impact outcomes and interpretations of geographic analyses.

Population

I. Geographical Analysis of Population

A. Basics of Demography

1. *Demography* is the study of human populations.

2. Geographers use demographic analysis to study the spatial distribution of humans and their movements.

3. The size, composition, and growth of a country's population affect its well-being.

B. Population Distribution

1. *Distribution* of a population is the pattern of people across Earth's surface.

2. Throughout human history, people have been *unevenly distributed*. Where people live is heavily influenced by physical conditions.

3. Populations are often clustered around sustaining resources, such as bodies of water and arable land. Fewer people live in deserts, for example.

   i. Approximately 75 percent of all humans live on only 5 percent of Earth's surface, the portion called the *ecumene.*

   ii. About 50 percent of people on Earth live in cities, whereas the other half live in rural areas.

   iii. This represents a shift in human settlement, since for most of human history, humans have lived predominantly in rural, not urban, spaces.

C. Global Population Distribution

1. Approximately 80 percent of Earth's population lives in poorer, less developed countries in Latin America, Africa, and Asia.

2. The only two countries to have more than 1 billion inhabitants are India and China.

3. The *largest concentration* of people on Earth is found in East Asia (China, Japan, Taiwan, North and South Korea).

   i. Nearly 1 in 4 humans live in this region.

   ii. Most Asians are subsistence farmers.

   ➤ Despite being agricultural and rural, they still live in high-density settlements, which is different from most of the Western world.

4. The *second-largest concentration* of people is in South Asia (India, Bangladesh, Sri Lanka, and Pakistan).

   i. Currently, India's rate of natural increase is higher than China's, making it probable that India will overtake China by 2030 as the world's most heavily populated country.

5. The *third-largest concentration* of people is in Europe, from the Atlantic to the Ural Mountains.

   i. This is related to the deep coal deposits that largely facilitated the population explosion associated with the Industrial Revolution of the 1800s.

   ii. In contrast to Asia, most Europeans are urban dwellers, living in cities. Remember that even though Europe has the highest *percentage* of urban residents, Asia still has the highest *number* of urban dwellers.

D. Population Density

1. *Density* is another tool geographers use to study population distribution. Density is simply the number of people in a particular land area. There are several types of density measurements.

2. *Arithmetic density* (also called population density) is the total number of people divided by the total land area.

   i.   For example, if 4.4 million people live in Minnesota, the area of which is 84,000 square miles, Minnesota has an arithmetic density of 4.4 million/84,000 = 52 people/square mile.

3. *Physiological density* is the number of people per unit of arable land. This is helpful to analyzing the amount of farmland available in the region.

   i.   For example, if the physiological population density of the U.S. is 340 people/square mile and Japan's is 7,000 people/square mile, this indicates that farmland in Japan is much more of a scarce commodity, given its population and land resources.

4. *Agricultural density* is the number of farmers per unit of arable land.

   i.   A very high agricultural density means that many farmers are on each piece of farmland.

   ii. A low agricultural density could suggest the presence of larger farms or more mechanized farming technology.

E. Population Equation

   1. Geographers analyze population trends at multiple scales, from global levels of inquiry to sub-global scales of inquiry.

   2. The *global demographic accounting equation* calculates global population change during an interval of time: $P_1 = P_0 + B - D$.

      i.   The formula means that the size of the population at the end of the interval of measurement, P_1, is found by taking the size of the population at the start of the interval of measurement, P_0, and adding the number of people born into the population, B, and subtracting the number of people in the population who died during the interval of measurement, D.

   3. The *sub-global (or regional) demographic accounting equation* is very similar, except it adds in immigration (I) and emigration (E): $P_1 = P_0 + B - D + I - E$.

    i.   *Immigration* refers to people coming into a country (or region).

    ii. *Emigration* refers to people leaving a country (or region).

F. Carrying Capacity and Overpopulation

1. A country's *carrying capacity* is the number of people the area can sustain or support.

2. Carrying capacity is a number that depends not only on available space, but also on the available technology, wealth, climate, and ability to bring in resources from other areas to support its people.

3. Improvements in a region's infrastructure can increase its carrying capacity. *Infrastructure* refers to support systems in a region, including housing, police forces, road systems, education, food supplies, and health care.

    i.   Saudi Arabia has developed desalination factories to remove salt from ocean water, thereby increasing the amount of available drinking water for its people.

    ii. Despite Israel's largely arid (dry) climate, it has developed advanced irrigation methods to create more arable lands to increase its farming output.

    iii. These innovative tactics have increased these regions' carrying capacities, despite a constant land area.

4. *Overpopulation* occurs when a region's population outgrows its carrying capacity.

5. Overpopulation is not always just a reflection of the natural resources, such as food and water, available in a region.

    ➤ For example, Japan has increased its carrying capacity to avoid overpopulation by developing trade relationships with other countries so Japan could import food for its people in exchange for Japanese technology.

6. Keep in mind, though, that some places are capable of producing more resources than they are able to harvest. Some less-developed countries could produce more food and resources, but their economic and technological infrastructures are not developed enough to increase production to meet their populations' needs.

i. The reasons for such *under-development* include colonial exploitation, educational and gender inequities, and inefficient economic and agricultural processes in place, among other factors.

In the **AP Human Geography** *exam, students are usually asked to provide examples in their FRQs. As you learn about key terms and concepts to prepare for the exam, be sure that you think about examples of each key term and concept that you could use in an FRQ response.*

G. Population Pyramids

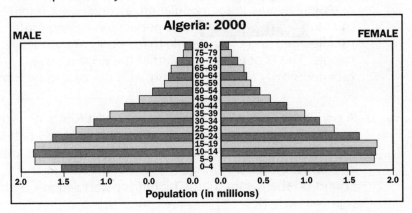

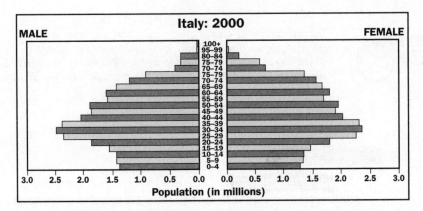

Examples of Population Pyramids

1. Demographers use *population pyramids* (age-sex structures) to evaluate the distribution of ages and genders in a given population.

2. A group of people of the same age is known as a *cohort*.

3. Each cohort is split between men and women on the pyramid.

4. The wider the base of the pyramid, the higher the percentage of young people exists in the population. This is generally an indication that the population will expand in the near future. This shape is more typical of developing countries, especially those in Sub-Saharan Africa.

5. The more *top-heavy* the pyramid, the higher the percentage of elderly people in the population, a condition referred to as a *graying population*, or a population having more middle-aged and older people than young, reproductive people. This is generally a sign that the population is growing slowly or even shrinking, as is the case in Italy and Russia.

6. A population pyramid can also help predict future growth of populations. Because a woman typically has a baby between 15 and 45 years (her fecund range), the higher the number of women in that age range (the wider the bar for that cohort on the pyramid), the higher the population's birth rate will likely be.

Test Tip

On one recent AP free-response question, students were given a population pyramid for a particular city and were asked to relate the information in the pyramid to patterns of urbanization and population distribution. Be sure you're able to do this.

H. Dependency Ratio

1. The *dependency ratio* is a helpful tool in analyzing the workforce and age distribution in a country. It compares those people not in the workforce with those in the labor force.

2. Generally, people aged 15 through 64 are considered *nondependent* because they can usually support themselves through work.

3. *Dependents* are usually people who are either older or younger than the working group. They depend on the workers (non-dependents) for their survival. Dependents are usually the elderly and children.

4. A high dependency ratio means that there are more people who are dependent than are working.

   i. This can lead to problems because there are fewer workers able to pay taxes and support programs needed to care for dependents, such as health care.

   ii. The dependency ratio is growing in Western Europe and the United States as the baby boomers age.

5. A graying population and rapid population growth are both related to an increasing dependency ratio.

   ➤ Some African regions have increasing dependency ratios because of high population growth rates, causing a high number of dependent children to outpace the number of working, non-dependent adults.

II. A Demographer's Toolbox

A. Key Measurements of Fertility and Mortality

   1. *Crude birth rate (CBR)*—number of live births per 1,000 people in a year.

   2. *Crude death rate (CDR)*—number of deaths per 1,000 people in a year.

      i. One interesting pattern exists in some more developed countries, where they are experiencing higher death rates than in less developed countries. This trend is related to the fact that some more-developed countries are experiencing "graying populations," with higher percentages of elderly people in their populations because of better health care, improved life expectancy, and lower birth rates among the younger generations.

3. *Rate of natural increase (RNI)*—the growth rate of a population, excluding immigration and emigration.

   i.   As of 2010, less developed regions are experiencing the highest rates of natural increase, whereas more developed regions have lower RNIs.

  ii.   The higher a population's RNI, the lower (or shorter) is the population's *doubling time*, or amount of time needed for the population to double in size.

4. *Infant mortality rate (IMR)*—number of infant deaths per 1,000 live births in a year.

   ➤   Infants who die before their first birthdays are also counted in IMR.

5. *Life expectancy (LE)*—average number of years to be lived by a person.

6. *Fecundity*—the ability of a woman to conceive. The fecund years are generally 15 to 45, but this range is expanding in many regions.

7. *General fertility rate (GFR)*—number of births per 1,000 women in their fecund years. This measure of fertility is more specific than the CBR.

8. *Total fertility rate (TFR)*—predicted number of births a woman will have as she passes through her fecund years. The 2010 global TFR was greater than 2.5, which means that a woman is likely to have between 2 and 3 children as she ages from 15 to 45.

B. Replacement Level Fertility

1. A TFR between 2.1–2.5 is considered *replacement level fertility*, meaning that the parents will produce, on average, only the number of children needed to replace themselves.

   ➤   The number is not a whole number because not everyone either reaches childbearing age or chooses/is able to have children. Therefore, some people need to have three to make up for those that either cannot or do not have children.

2. Replacement-level fertility rates can lead to *zero population growth*, when the population size remains the same from year to year.

III. Population Growth and Decline Over Space and Time

A. Population Explosion

1. Over the last three hundred years, Earth has experienced a dramatic population increase, which some would call a *population explosion.*

2. Currently, the global human population of nearly 6.9 billion is increasing at an *exponential growth rate,* which means that the more people that are added, the faster the population is growing.

3. Exponential growth is different from *linear (or arithmetic) growth,* which is a fixed rate of growth. For example, in 1750, the population was about 700 million people. In just 260 years, the population has grown to exceed 6 billion.

B. Historical Trends in Population Change

1. Approximately 10,000–12,000 years ago, the *First Agricultural Revolution* empowered humans with the ability to domesticate crops and build settlements through farming, rather than always hunting and gathering on the move.

2. Thereafter, cities began to develop and the population began to grow at faster rates.

3. In the 1700s, the *Industrial Revolution,* which diffused from England, facilitated the growth of new technologies and industry.

4. Alongside this industrial shift was the *Second Agricultural Revolution,* which improved crop fertilization and storage capacities.

5. These two forces—industrialization and improved food capacities—worked together to support the rapid, Western European population surge that developed. Such a pattern spread to Eastern European regions and to North America.

6. In industrializing areas, urban populations began to boom and cities rapidly became overcrowded as people moved from rural areas to find factory jobs.

C. Theories of Population Growth

1. In response to the rapid urban population growth during the Western European industrialization, British theorist *Thomas Malthus* wrote in his 1798 publication, *An Essay on the Principle of Population*, that the world's population growth would exceed its carrying capacity.

   i. Malthus argued that the population was growing exponentially (or geometrically), while its food supply was only growing arithmetically. In other words, the population was growing at a faster rate than the food supply.

   ii. Malthus advocated for *positive checks* on population growth, such as birth control and celibacy. He also warned of *negative checks* on population growth, such as starvation and disease.

   iii. Malthus was also a minister, so part of his argument was based on the moral issue that people should abstain because that is the morally correct thing to do. He linked overpopulation, in part, to immortality.

   iv. Critics of Malthusian theory argue that Malthus failed to predict agricultural innovations that could increase the rate and quantity of food production, such as genetic modification of foods.

   v. Contemporary advocates of Malthus (called *Neo-Malthusians*) call for regions not to exceed their carrying capacities.

2. *Karl Marx* wrote that the problem was not population growth rates, but was related to the unequal distribution of wages and resources.

3. *Ester Boserup* believed that overpopulation could be avoided by increasing the number of subsistence farmers.

D. Population Policies

1. *Pro-natalist* (or *expansive*) *policies* by a government promote reproduction and bigger families.

   ➤ A tax break for families with children is a pro-natalist policy since it encourages and rewards reproduction.

2. *Anti-natalist* (or *restrictive*) *policies* discourage reproduction and try to reduce population growth rates.

   i. Some governments offer tax breaks and rewards to citizens for getting sterilized, which halts one's ability to reproduce.

   ii. China's *one-child policy*, which punished families for having more than one child, was an anti-natalist policy.

   iii. Harsh anti-natalist policies, such as the one-child policy, can lead to *female infanticide*, when families abort or kill female newborns because male children are preferred.

   iv. Such harshly anti-natalist policies can contribute to *imbalanced sex ratios*, when the number of males is unequal to the number of females.

E. Population Projections for the Future

1. The United Nations (UN) devised various *growth scenarios* to predict future population growth.

   i. Its *low-growth scenario* predicts that Earth's population will begin declining, reaching 7.5 billion in 2050 and 5.1 billion by 2100.

   ii. Its *high-growth scenario* predicts a global population of 11 billion by 2050, rising to 16 billion by 2100.

      iii. Its *medium-growth scenario,* which most demographers accept, predicts 9 billion by 2050 and 9.4 billion by 2100.

    2. At a *2004 UN Conference on Population,* UN leaders identified *empowering women* through improved educational and economic opportunities as key to reducing global RNI.

      ➤ More choices for women translates into lower RNI because women can, if they choose, gain self-worth outside of having children.

F. Epidemic vs. Pandemic

    1. A *pandemic* is a disease, such as HIV/AIDS, that affects very large numbers of people, often at a global level.

    2. An *epidemic* is a disease affecting a more local region acutely.

    3. In 2010, nearly 42 million people, or 1.2 percent of the world's adult population, were living with HIV/AIDS, with 5 million new infections occurring each year.

    4. In sub-Saharan Africa, some HIV/AIDS epidemics are still expanding. As of 2010, nearly 20 percent of adults in some sub-Saharan regions were infected with HIV/AIDS.

    5. Africa is the *epicenter,* or region at the center of impact, of the global HIV/AIDS pandemic.

    6. Asia is also rapidly confronting its own HIV/AIDS crisis. In 2010, approximately 7 million Asians were living with the virus, indicating an infection rate which is among the fastest in the world.

      ➤ As seen in other regions facing HIV/AIDS, factors such as drug use, poverty, insufficient health care, and discrimination of homosexuals have contributed to Asia's HIV/AIDS crisis.

G. Demographic Momentum

    1. Sometimes called *hidden* momentum, *demographic momentum* occurs in many underdeveloped countries when

the population continues to grow even after replacement-level fertility is reached (when TFR is between 2.1–2.5).

2. This can happen when the population pyramids have such a wide base and a narrow top. Therefore, when large numbers of young people start having babies, even if only two per couple, that new generation of births surpasses the number of older people dying.

3. Because many of the children are expected to live longer with improvements in health care, there can be positive population growth even if families are reproducing at replacement level. This is why it is called "hidden."

4. Hidden momentum can make it difficult for some countries with wide population bases, like India, to reach zero population growth.

IV. The Demographic Transition Model (DTM)

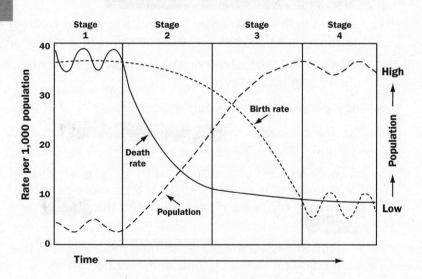

Demographic Transition Model

A. **The Basics of the Model**

   1. The *demographic transition model (DTM)* is a geographic model that explains and predicts changes in population (or demographic) growth.

   2. The DTM predicts changes in CBR, CDR, and RNI as a country "transitions" through economic development.

   3. It is based on the assumption that economics drive demographic change and that all countries will pass through four stages of demographic transition.

Test Tip

> *The DTM is a key model, appearing on both released exams and numerous FRQs in various forms. Thinking through the DTM, its applications, and its limitations is very important for your focused preparation.*

B. **Stage 1: Low Growth (High Stationary) Stage**

   1. CBR and CDR are extremely high in stage 1, thus creating a low RNI (since CBR and CDR are nearly equal, though high).

   2. CBR and CDR fluctuate, though minimally, because of disease, famine, and war.

   3. Most people in stage 1 countries are subsistence farmers.

   4. This stage is known as *stationary* or *in equilibrium* because CBR and CDR are nearly equal and are not moving.

   5. All countries have progressed past stage 1, largely through the diffusion of medical technology from more-developed countries in the late 20th century during the *medical revolution*.

      ➤ With improved medicine reaching more places in the medical revolution, people in these poorer regions began having longer life expectancies, which coupled with the already high birth rates in these regions, led to higher population growth rates.

C. Stage 2: High Growth (Expanding) Stage

1. CBR is still high, but CDR declines as new health care systems, such as improved medical supplies, arrive.

2. CBR still remains high because most families are still subsistence farmers and because the CBR is often a deeply-rooted cultural tradition and cannot be easily changed.

3. Because the CBR remains high and the CDR declines, the RNI increases and population expansion is at a high rate.

4. Many less developed countries are currently in Stage 2.

   ➤ For example, Kenya's high CBR of 32 per 1000 but low CDR of 14 per 1000 yield a high growth rate.

D. Stage 3: Moderate Growth (Expanding) Stage

1. The CBR begins to fall because families decide to lower their birth rates in response to changing conditions, such as moving to cities to work in factories and improved health conditions, which cause children to live longer.

2. Women also have more opportunities in industrializing economies that often characterize stage 2 conditions.

3. RNI is decreasing (because the CBR is dropping closer to the already lower CDR), but it is still greater than zero. Thus, the population is still expanding in size.

4. Most Latin American and Asian countries remain in stage 3 at moderate growth.

E. Stage 4: Low Growth (Low Stationary) Stage

1. The CBR falls and meets the CDR at equally low levels, thus reaching equilibrium, or a stationary status.

2. Because the CBR and CDR are reaching equilibrium, the RNI stabilizes at a lower level, close to zero-population growth.

3. Some demographers propose a fifth stage that would demonstrate graying population trends. In such a proposed stage, the CBR would drop below the CDR, causing a population decline, or a *negative RNI.*

4. Many Western European countries are at the end of stage 4's zero population growth equilibrium and pushing towards a potential 5th stage, if one exists. Japan is also facing a graying population.

F. Some Criticisms of the DTM

1. Critics of the DTM point to the fact that it is based on England's demographic transition as it moved from being a subsistence agricultural economy to an industrialized society.

2. Critics do not believe all countries will pass through the same demographic transition pattern as was seen in England's history and depicted in the DTM.

3. Critics also point to the fact that the DTM is based on 19th century population change, which involved millions of people, not billions, as seen today.

4. Also, England progressed from stage 2 to stage 3 in about 100 years, whereas modern countries often experience more rapid demographic transition.

   ➤ Several South-east Asian countries, such as Hong Kong and Malaysia, developed at a much faster rate than did the early industrialized countries on which the DTM is based.

V. Epidemiologic Transition Model

1. The *epidemiologic transition model* (ETM) is related to the demographic transition model because the ETM focuses on identifying and explaining the causes of death in countries in each stage of the DTM.

2. The ETM predicts that the primary causes of death in countries in stage 1 of the DTM will be famine, drought, and pandemics such as the bubonic plague.

   ➤ Stage 1 in the ETM is known as the "Age of Pestilence and Famine."

3. In countries in stage 2, known as the "Age of Receding Pandemics," the primary causes of death will be diseases associated with overcrowding and urbanization, since most countries in stage 2 of demographic transition are undergoing industrialization and urbanization (movement into cities).

> ➤ Diseases such as cholera are related to overcrowding and urbanization.

4. Countries in stages 3 and 4 are approaching modern economies and health care systems. Thus, the ETM predicts that the primary causes of death in countries in these stages are likely to be related to longer life expectancies, such as heart attacks and cancers.

> ➤ Stage 3 is known in the model as the "Age of Degenerative and Man-made Diseases," whereas Stage 4 is known as the "Stage of Delayed Degenerative Diseases."

5. Some demographers also call for a fifth stage in the ETM, one in which the diseases associated with stage 1 countries, such as the plague and smallpox, reappear.

> ➤ This is based on the fact that residents in such modern countries can come into contact with diseases such as smallpox still present in less developed regions and reintroduce these diseases back into their home country's populations.

Test Tip

As one of the released exams shows, students were asked which region had the highest <u>number</u> of urban residents. Even though Europe may have a higher percentage of urban dwellers, Asia's sheer population size gives it the highest <u>number</u> of urban residents. Be sure to read each question very carefully—try underlining important terms, like "number" in this example.

Migration

I. Migration

A. Spatial Interaction and Friction of Distance

1. If you've noticed, it seems as if the interconnectedness of the world is increasing. Some think we are actually getting closer together, even though our real distance remains the same.

2. Distance is not the barrier to communication and travel that it once was for most people.

   ➤ The difficulties we have overcoming these spatial and temporal barriers are commonly referred to as the *friction of distance.*

3. The process of coming together and having more contact with each other, even though real distance remains the same, is called *space-time compression.*

4. The friction of distance is being reduced through space-time compression, and as a result, spatial interaction is increasing.

   ➤ *Spatial interaction* is simply the interaction between two places, whether through communication, economic transaction, migration, or travel.

B. Migration

1. As we become more linked together, our ability to move across Earth's surface is increasingly more accessible for more people.

2. *Migration* is the process of permanently moving from your home region and crossing an administrative border or boundary, such as between counties, states, or countries.

C. Push and Pull Factors

1. The decision to migrate is often based on thoughtful consideration by the people choosing to make the journey.

2. Often, migration decisions are based on a combination of push and pull factors influencing a person's movement.

3. *Push factors* are the negative influences that make a person want to move away, such as high taxes, high crime rates, and abusive governments, among others.

4. *Pull factors* are the positive influences that pull a person toward a particular place, such as affordable real estate, good schools, and clean parks.

5. The assignment of what is a push and what is a pull factor can be highly personal. For example, being near family members may be a positive pull factor to one person, but it might be a push factor for another!

D. Migration Streams

1. Migration patterns often give clues to what is happening in various parts of the world.

2. A *migration stream* is a pathway from a place of origin to a destination.

Test Tip

On a previous exam, students were asked to analyze a map showing migration streams. Keep in mind that migration streams are usually shown on maps as arrows; the thicker the arrow, the larger the group of migrants moving in that pathway.

3. Places attracting lots of migrants must have *high place desirability,* possession of positive features making people want to move there.

4. If a place has more immigrants (moving into it) than emigrants (leaving it), the place has a *net in-migration.*

5. Likewise, if a place has more emigrants than immigrants, the place has a *net out-migration.*

    i.   A net in-migration usually indicates that an area has high place desirability; net out-migration usually indicates the opposite.

    ii. If hordes of people are emigrating from a place, perhaps something is pushing those masses of people out of that place.

    iii. North America, Oceania, and Europe are experiencing net in-migration.

    iv. Asia, Africa, and Latin America are experiencing net out-migration.

6. Usually, where there is a migration stream, there is a *migration counterstream* of people moving back to the place of origin from the new place.

    i.   Counterstreams can be caused by many factors, sometimes legal, economic, or personal.

         ➤ Sadly, the out-migration of Jews from Nazi Germany had a small, tragic counterstream back into Germany because of their capture and forced return by border officials in other countries refusing to allow Jews shelter from Nazi oppression.

         ➤ More recent examples involve Mexicans moving back to Mexico from the U.S. for various reasons and Indians from all over the world returning to India to take advantage of the growing economy.

E. Chain Migration

1. Migration streams often develop because of information exchange.

    ➤ People in the place of origin may hear of great opportunities in a new place, may have family members in a new community, or may be seeing advertisements for a new place.

2. *Chain migration* occurs when people migrate to be with other people who migrated before them and with whom they feel some linkage, whether it is familial, religious, ethnic, cultural, or some other type of connection.

F. Voluntary versus Forced Migration

1. *Voluntary migration* occurs when migrants have an option of whether or not to move.

2. *Involuntary* (or *forced*) *migration* is when migrants are pushed from their land.

➤ The largest forced migration occurred with the North Atlantic slave trade, which forced nearly 30 million Africans from their homes to migrate to the Americas.

3. *Refugees* are migrants fleeing some form of persecution or abuse.

➤ *International refugees* flee their country and move to another country, while *intranational* (or *internally displaced peoples*) *refugees* abandon their homes but remain in their country.

G. Some Major Regions of Dislocation and Refugees

1. Sub-Saharan Africa:

➤ Millions of people fled Rwanda and the Congo in response to tribal or ethnic conflicts.

➤ In the Darfur region of northeastern Sudan, religious and ethnic tensions between the North and South, Muslims and animists, and the government and rebels have led to massive dislocation.

➤ Zaire, Tanzania, Uganda, Liberia, Sierra Leone, Angola, and Burundi have also seen large numbers of war-related refugees.

2. The Middle East (which many argue includes North Africa):

➤ A large stream of ethnic Palestinians migrated into neighboring countries such as Jordan, Syria, and Egypt after the formation of Israel.

➤ Additional dislocations include the Kurdish people from the former Iraq and Afghanistan's citizens during the Soviet occupation in the 1980s.

3. Europe:

➤ The fall of Yugoslavia in the Balkans led to the largest refugee crisis in Europe since WWII. Nearly 7 million refugees fled their homes during this conflict.

4. Southeast Asia:

➤ The Vietnam War created nearly 2 million refugees.

➤ Cambodia's violent governmental transition uprooted nearly 30,000 refugees.

➤ The dictatorial government of Burma (now Myanmar) has dislocated thousands.

5. South Asia: In addition to Afghani refugees fleeing into neighboring Pakistan, Sri Lanka has seen nearly 1 million of its citizens dislocated by a feud with the Sinhalese government.

II. Major Migrations at Different Scales

A. Waves of Immigration in the U.S.

1. The U.S. has seen three major waves of immigration, each originating from a different part of the world.

2. In the colonial era, from early 1600s–1776, Europe and Africa were the primary sources of migrants, both voluntary and involuntary, to the New World.

➤ Many Europeans were fleeing political and religious persecution, while Africans were forced to come to the Americas as slaves.

3. The 19th century saw continued migration from Europe. Before the 1840s, most immigrants in America originated in England, but in the 1840s and 1850s, massive numbers of Irish and Germans migrated across the Atlantic in search of opportunity.

> ➤ More than 4.2 million people migrated to the U.S. during this wave, more than twice that since colonization.

Test Tip

Students were asked on a previous exam FRQ to relate the demographic transition model to emigration from Europe during 1800—1920 and to immigration from North Africa to Europe in the late 20th century. It is crucial to draw connections between trends in demographic transition, economic and historical issues, and migration patterns.

4. Immigration slumped during the Civil War but surged again in the early 20th century, fueled by the *Industrial Revolution*.

   i. New migrants in the 1900s came not just from northern and western Europe but now from areas like Italy, Austria-Hungary, and Russia.

   ii. Unrestricted immigration to the U.S. was halted by the *Quota Act of 1921*, which allowed higher numbers of immigrants from European countries and discriminated against Asians and other regions.

5. During the Great Depression and WWII, immigration to the U.S. dropped off dramatically, but reached new heights again in the 1980s and 1990s.

   > ➤ During the 1970s and 1980s, Asia was the leading source of immigration to the U.S.

   > ➤ By the late 1980s, Latin America was the leading source of immigrants to the U.S.

   > ➤ Some U.S. immigrants are *guest workers*, temporarily allowed in the U.S. on work permits. Many U.S. immigrants send *remittances*, which are money transactions sent home by guest workers to family

members in their home countries. Guest workers perform many different types of economic functions, from farming to working at large corporations and universities.

B. Internal Migration

1. *Internal migration* is movement within a country, as opposed to *international (or external) migration,* which is movement outside a country.

2. There are two types of internal migration—interregional and intraregional migration.

   i. *Interregional migration* is moving from one region in the country to another region in the country.

   ii. *Intraregional migration* is moving within a region, such as from a city to a suburb.

3. As industrialization built up cities in the U.S., more and more Americans migrated from farms to cities in a pattern of urban migration (intraregional migration). A counterstream developed as people left the crowded cities for suburbs.

   ➤ Recently, an increasing number of U.S. city dwellers have been moving back to the solace of rural areas in a trend known as *counterurbanization.*

Test Tip

It is important to think about the interrelationship between this chapter, giving you key information on migration, and the later chapter on urban spaces. Trends in urbanization are directly related to internal migration and suburbanization.

C. Shifting Center of U.S. Population

1. The U.S. migration pattern has shifted its center of population patterns consistently westward and in a southerly direction.

2. During the *Great Migration,* which occurred as the U.S. fought in WWI, many southern African Americans moved north in search of industrial jobs that were opening up because of the war.

3. By the 1970s, however, more African Americans were returning to the South than were moving north, a migration stream that increased as U.S. factories closed down.

4. This closing (or "rusting") of industrial-era factories in the U.S. is forming a *Rustbelt* in the Northeast and a *Sunbelt* in the South, as migrants move to take advantage of the "sunny" economy and opportunity.

III.   Predicting and Explaining Migration

A. Migration Selectivity

1. The decision to migrate often fits into a predictable pattern based on age, income, and other socio-economic factors.

2. *Migration selectivity* is the evaluation of how likely someone is to migrate based on personal, social, and economic factors.

3. Age is the most influential factor in migration selectivity.

   ➤ Americans are most likely to move between the ages of 18 and 30, the time in which they leave their parents' homes, find employment, attend college, go to war, and so on.

4. Education is also a factor in migration selectivity.

   i.   Typically, the more educated people are, the more likely they are to make long-distance moves because of their increased knowledge of more-distant opportunities and greater job qualifications.

   ii. Some places experiencing net out-migration suffer from *brain-drain,* when the most educated workers leave for more attractive destinations.

    iii. The Appalachian region in Kentucky often loses its most talented cohort of young people to brain drain.

    iv. Some geographers are using the term *brain-gain* to describe regions that invest little in education yet see educated workers still migrate there, nonetheless.

B. Ravenstein's Migration "Laws"

  1. In the late 1800s, British geographer Ernst Ravenstein identified 11 generalizations about migration, some of which still apply to modern conditions.

  2. Here are some of Ravenstein's most important generalizations:

    i. The majority of migrants travel short distances. Most migrants travel in *step migration,* when a person has a long-distance goal in mind and achieves it in small steps.

    ii. Migrants who are traveling a long way tend to move to larger cities rather than smaller cities.

      ➤ Keep in mind that Ravenstein was researching in the 1800s, when England was experiencing the Industrial Revolution, pulling people to mega-cities like London and Manchester.

    iii. Rural residents are more likely to migrate than are urban residents.

      ➤ Again, during Ravenstein's era, many rural residents were packing up and moving to cities for industrial jobs and brighter opportunities.

      ➤ Today, this generalization varies by region. China, which is currently industrializing, is experiencing this trend.

      ➤ Yet counter-urbanization is a noted trend in the U.S., as city dwellers are leaving crowded urban places for the suburbs and more rural spaces.

iv. Families are less likely to migrate across national borders than are young adults.

> ➤ Ravenstein asserted that it is easier for single people to migrate than it is for whole families.

v. Every migration stream creates a counterstream.

C. The Gravity Model

1. Geographers use the *gravity model* to estimate spatial interaction and movement between two places. It is known as the "gravity" model because it resembles Sir Isaac Newton's theory of gravitational pull.

2. Essentially, the gravity model predicts that larger places attract more migrants than smaller places, just as larger planets have more gravitational pull.

3. It also predicts that closer places attract more migrants than more distant places.

4. In all, the gravity model proposes an equation that balances distance and size in trying to predict spatial patterns.

> ➤ For example, the model could be used to predict higher numbers of Mexicans choosing to migrate to the U.S. than to England because of friction of distance factors; the U.S. is simply closer for Mexicans than is England.

5. The model can be helpful for predicting migration patterns, but it has limitations. It does not factor in migration selectivity factors, such as age and education level. Human behavior does not always fit into predicted patterns.

D. Zelinksy's Model of Migration Transition

1. Wilbur Zelinsky's *model of migration transition* explains and predicts migration changes in a country based on the country's stage in the demographic transition model.

2. Zelinsky's model predicts that people from countries in stage 1 of the demographic transition model are searching on a local basis for necessities but only moving on a temporary basis in their search for food and shelter materials.

3. People in countries in stage 2 of the demographic transition model are experiencing such high rates of natural increase that overtaxing of resources and limited opportunities push people to migrate to more developed countries.

➤ Many North Africans are currently emigrating from their stage 2 countries for new horizons in more developed western European countries, where jobs and opportunities are often thought to be available.

4. In stage 4 countries, most migration is intraregional, with people moving from cities to suburbs and back.

E. Short-Term Local Movements and Activity Spaces

1. In addition to studying migration, geographers also analyze people's daily movements that are not classified as migration.

2. The area in which you travel on a daily basis is known as your *activity space.*

i. Often, improved transportation technology, such as planes, trains, and cars, increases the size of one's activity space.

ii. Modern communication technology, such as smartphones and GPS, are believed to impact our daily activity space.

3. There are various classifications of this shorter-term, impermanent movement:

i. *Cyclic movement* occurs during your daily routine from your home and back. Commuting from one's home to work and back is a form of cyclic movement.

ii. *Seasonal movement* is a form of cyclic movement that involves leaving your home region for a short time in response to a change of season.

iii. *Periodic movement* involves longer periods of stay, such as serving in the military or attending college.

F. Intervening Opportunities and Obstacles

1. Often in the process of making a long journey, people encounter an *intervening opportunity,* a place they like so much along their journey that it keeps them from continuing on to the planned, final destination.

2. An *intervening obstacle* is a barrier in a migratory journey that prevents the migrant from reaching the planned, final destination. Financial problems, immigration requirements, and wars are examples of intervening obstacles.

Cultural Patterns and Processes

I. Concepts of Culture

A. Cultural Geography

1. *Cultural geography* is defined as the study of people's lifestyles, their creations, and their relationships to the Earth and the supernatural.

2. It is a field within human geography that looks at how and why culture is expressed in different ways in different places.

3. It involves the study of both material and non-material aspects of culture.

4. *Material components of culture* include tangible artifacts that can be physically left behind, such as clothing and architecture.

5. *Non-material components of culture* include the thoughts and ideas of a people, such as their religion and laws.

B. Cultural Landscape

1. Sometimes referred to as the "built landscape," the *cultural landscape* is the physical imprint a culture makes on the environment. Buildings, artwork, and even music are all examples of cultural elements woven into a people's cultural landscape.

2. *Carl Sauer*, a famous 20th century geographer, championed the study of the cultural landscape. He asserted that wherever a human culture exists, a cultural landscape exists as that culture's unique "fingerprint" on their space on the Earth.

3. *Cultural ecology* is the study of human–environment interaction and all that results from the interplay.

C. Sequent Occupancy

1. *Sequent occupancy* is the theory that a place can be occupied by different groups of people, and each group leaves its imprint on the place from which the next group learns.

   ➤ For example, the Romans, Saxons, Vikings, and other groups conquered England over a period of 3,000 years, taking over the same territory, changing it to fit their needs, and in the process, leaving behind an imprint for future occupiers to learn and inherit.

II. Geographic Theories Explaining Human–Environment Interaction

In studying human-environment interaction, cultural geographers encounter the question, "Does the Earth make humans take the actions they do?" Several geographic theories have attempted to answer this question.

A. Environmental Determinism

1. *Environmental determinism* is a theory developed as early as the Greeks that argues that human behavior is controlled (or determined) by the physical environment.

2. A geographer believing in environmental determinism would likely argue that "ideal" climates *cause* more productive citizens, such as the Egyptian region near the Nile River. Harsher climates, as in freezing Siberia, do not foster productivity.

B. Possibilism

1. *Possibilism* is a theory that developed as a counterargument to environmental determinism. It argues that the natural environment places limits on the set of choices (or possibilities) available to people.

2. According to possibilism, people, not the environment, propel human cultural development, though the environment limits the set of choices available to them.

C. Cultural Determinism

1. Many geographers have discounted possibilism in favor of *cultural determinism,* the theory that the environment places no restrictions on humans whatsoever.

2. Cultural determinism argues that the only restrictions humans face are the ones they create for themselves. For example, one might think the environment restricts placing a golf course (which requires extensive watering) in a desert. But what if water was piped in from long distances and seeds were engineered to require less watering? An analysis of this from the angle of cultural determinism would argue that the only restriction on building the golf course would come from a cultural, not environmental, restriction.

D. Political Ecology

1. *Political ecology* also attempts to answer why human cultures interact with environments in the ways they do. It asserts that the government of a region affects the environment in that region, which in turn affects the choices (and possibilities) available to the people in the region.

   ➤ Think of how zoning laws regulate the possibilities for building different types of buildings in different parts of the city. Even if you wanted to build a church in an industrial area of your city, you may be restricted from doing so because of the zoning laws.

III. Layers of Culture

A. Culture Traits

1. A *culture trait* is a single attribute of a culture, such as bowing to show respect.

2. Culture traits are not necessarily unique to one group of people. For example, bowing out of respect is a trait of Japanese culture, but cultures outside of Japan also bow out of respect.

B. Culture Complex

1. The combination of all culture traits creates a unique set of traits called a *culture complex*.

2. No two cultures in the world have the exact same combination of traits in their culture complexes.

C. Culture Systems

1. When many culture complexes share particular traits, such as bowing out of respect, those complexes can merge to form a *culture system*.

   ➤ For example, people living in northern Germany speak with a different accent than Germans living in the southern region. But these two complexes share many other traits that can be fused into the German culture system.

D. Culture Regions

1. While we have learned about formal, functional, and perceptual regions, another type of region is the *culture region*, drawn around places and peoples with similarities in their culture systems.

2. People in culture regions often share a sense of common culture and *regional identity,* or emotional attachment to the group of people and places associated with a particular culture region.

3. But the boundaries of culture regions are often defined by perceptions and opinions from people within the shared culture and from observers outside of them. Therefore, the definition of a culture region is often based in perspective.

> ➤ For example, the cultural region of the "South" is defined by people's beliefs and attitudes about various topics and cultural symbols (such as grits, a type of food some argue is "southern.")

E. Culture Realms

1. A *culture (or geographic) realm* is formed through the fusing together of culture regions that share enough in common to be merged together.

2. Commonly accepted culture realms include the Anglo-American realm, Latin American realm, European realm, and the Sino-Japanese realm. As with culture regions, there are often no fixed boundaries for a culture realm; rather, such boundaries are grounded in perceptions.

Test Tip

It is very important that you think through the interrelationship of concepts in Human Geography. For example, thinking through how elements of culture impact humans' use of land and space was critical in answering a free-response question on a previous AP exam that asked students to analyze how different cultures treat sacred space. Students who recognized that aspects of religious culture impact humans' use of land performed better on this question than those who had not thought through these important connections.

IV. Cultural Diffusion

A. Cultural Diffusion and Spatial Diffusion

1. People's material and nonmaterial creations spread across time and space, moving to new places and being carried through generations.

2. *Cultural diffusion* is the spread of a people's culture across space.

3. The spread of any phenomenon (such as a disease) across space is called *spatial diffusion.*

4. There are two categories of diffusion: expansion and relocation.

B. Expansion Diffusion

1. In *expansion diffusion,* the cultural component (or phenomenon) spreads outward to new places while remaining strong in its original *hearth,* or place of origin. For example, Islam spread from its hearth area in Saudi Arabia to other areas around and outside of its hearth while remaining strong in Medina and Mecca.

2. There are several forms of expansion diffusion.

   i. *Stimulus expansion diffusion* occurs when the innovative (or original) idea diffuses from its hearth outward, but the original idea is changed by the new adopters.

      ➤ For example, iced tea diffused south, but the southerners made it "sweeter" to become "sweet tea." The original idea diffused but was adapted to meet the needs of the new adopters.

   ii. *Hierarchical expansion diffusion* occurs when the diffusion innovation or concept spreads from a place or person of power (or susceptibility to the diffusing phenomenon) to another in a leveled (or hierarchical) pattern.

      ➤ For example, hip-hop music diffused in a hierarchical pattern, spreading from a few large inner cities to other large inner cities and then to smaller inner cities, and finally to more suburban and rural places.

iii. *Contagious expansion diffusion* occurs when numerous places or people near the point of origin become adopters (or infected, in the case of a disease).

➤ An example of the effects of contagious expansion diffusion is shown in the spread of tuberculosis from its point of origin to surrounding people who happened to be near where it started.

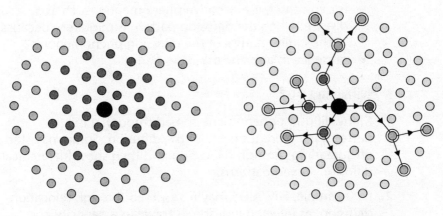

A. Contagious Diffusion   **B. Hierarchical Diffusion**

LEGEND		
● Hearth	● Early diffusion	○ Later diffusion
○ Important person or place		○ No diffusion

Contagious versus Hierarchial Diffusion

C. Relocation Diffusion

1. *Relocation diffusion* involves the actual movement of the original adopters from their point of origin (or hearth) to a new place.

2. In expansion diffusion, it is the innovation (or disease) that does the moving; in relocation diffusion, the people pick up and move, carrying the phenomenon that is diffusing with them to a new place.

3. A form of relocation diffusion is *migrant diffusion,* in which the innovation spreads and lasts only a brief time in the newly adopting place. The number of fans for a pop band often swells in the city where the group is performing but then weakens once the concert ends and the group moves on to its next performance city, where there is again a rise in the number of fans grouped in the place.

> ➤ It is sometimes hard to find the heart of a phenomenon (or epicenter, if a negative phenomenon, such as a disease) when the diffusion pattern is migratory because of the fading nature of the diffusing phenomenon's presence in any one place.

D. A Mix of Patterns

1. Many diffusing phenomena spread through a mix of patterns in different phases of the diffusion. Some may start off spreading through relocation and then show hierarchical diffusion spread patterns.

2. For example, HIV/AIDS may first spread through relocation diffusion, as infected individuals travel to a new city and infect (albeit unknowingly) others in the city with the virus.

3. After being transplanted initially through relocation diffusion, if the newly infected individuals in the new region spread HIV/AIDS first to the most susceptible group (perhaps those not practicing safe sex), then to a broader base, then the diffusion pattern shows hierarchical effects.

4. If the virus also was spreading not just through levels of susceptibility but also just by proximity to the new epicenter, then HIV/AIDS also was showing contagious expansion effects.

E. Culture Hearths

Hypothesized Ancient Hearth	Direction of Diffusion of Civilization from Ancient Hearth
Andean America (near Andes Mountains in South America)	Eastward direction throughout South America
Mesoamerica	Eastern and western North America
West Africa	Throughout Africa
Nile River valley	Throughout Africa and Southwest Asia
Mesopotamia	Throughout Southwest Asia, Europe, Central and East Asia, West Africa
Indus River valley	Throughout Southwest, Central, and East Asia
Ganges River delta	Throughout South, Southeast, and Southwest Asia
Wei and Huang rivers (China)	Throughout East and Southeast Asia

1. *Culture hearths* are areas where innovations in culture began, such as where agriculture, government, and urbanization originated.

2. Culture hearths were the sources of human civilization.

3. Ancient culture hearths are believed to have developed in places with the capacity for innovation, all near sources of water and arable land.

4. Often, similar innovations are invented in different hearths without any interaction, such as when agricultural innovation occurred in East Asia and in Mesopotamia. This is known as *independent innovation* (or invention).

5. Geographer Torsten Hagerstrand's research theorized that innovations of all kinds tend to diffuse from their hearths in stages. First, innovations gain acceptance in their origin, then begin to spread rapidly outward from their origin, eventually slowing and reaching maximum dispersal and saturation.

V. **Diffusion S-Curve**

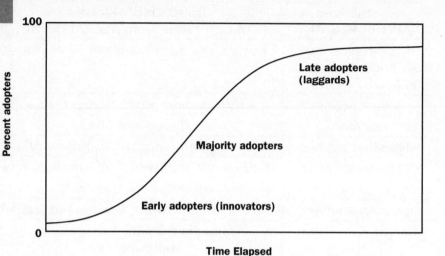

Diffusion S-Curve

1. Hagerstrand's research led geographers to see that diffusion often follows an *S-curve* pattern, with stages of early adopters, majority adopters, and then late adopters.

2. It is called an "S-curve" pattern because the graph showing the diffusion trend over time resembles the letter "S."

   ➤ This term is derived from Roger's Diffusion of Innovation Theory.

   ➤ Think about the pattern of cell phone diffusion. Initially, a small group of people who could afford them and knew about them adopted cell phones (*early adopters*).

   ➤ Once more people learned about them and prices fell, a much faster rate of adoption of cell phones developed (*the majority adopter stage*).

   ➤ During the majority adopter phase, most people who were susceptible (or likely) to be affected by the diffusing phenomena (cell phones) became adopters.

> ➤ In the last stage of the S-curve diffusion pattern, the rate of adoption slows down and *"late adopters"* (or laggards), who had not yet bought cell phones, purchased them.

VI. Cultural Convergence and Divergence

A. Cultural Convergence vs. Divergence

1. *Cultural convergence* occurs when two cultures adopt each other's traits and become more alike.

2. *Cultural divergence* occurs when two cultures become increasingly different, often when one group moves away from the territory of one culture group.

B. Acculturation, Assimilation, and Transculturation

1. *Acculturation* occurs when two cultures come into contact with one another and the "weaker" of the two adopts traits from the more dominant culture.

2. Sometimes acculturation leads to *assimilation*, when the original traits of the weaker culture are completely replaced by the traits of the more dominant culture.

3. A "weaker" culture (or less dominant) often refers to a culture that, comparatively, has less political power or less acceptance by the mainstream.

3. Sometimes *transculturation* occurs when two cultures of just about equal power or influence meet and exchange ideas or traits without the domination seen in acculturation and assimilation.

VII. **Ethnicity and Race**

A. Ethnicity

1. *Ethnicity* is a core component of cultural identity and relates to sets of norms that people create to define "their group" through actual or perceived shared cultural traits.

➤ Some examples of shared cultural traits a people may use to define a common ethnicity may be language, religion, and/or nationality.

2. Territory is often a unifying trait for ethnicities.

➤ Albanians' attachment to Albania is an example of how territory unified this ethnic, cultural group.

B. Separation of Ethnic Groups

1. Ethnic groups may be spatially divided. Many ethnic Albanians lived in the Serb-ruled region of Kosovo, a neighboring region that became a flash-point of conflict in the 1990s, when Yugoslavia disintegrated.

2. A *ghetto* is a region in which an ethnic minority is forced to live by economic, legal, or governmental pressures.

3. An *ethnic enclave* is a place in which an ethnic minority is concentrated, sometimes in the form of a ghetto.

i. The term *enclave* can indicate a place in which a minority group is concentrated and surrounded by another ethnic group, which can be unwelcoming or hostile (but not always).

ii. A *barrio* is a Spanish-speaking ethnic enclave (or neighborhood) in a city, although the term is sometimes used with negative racial connotations.

C. Race

1. *Race* refers to a classification system of humans based on skin color and other physical characteristics.

2. What differentiates race and ethnicity is not always clear, but ethnicity is usually seen to incorporate more than just race.

➤ Race is biological and not chosen, whereas ethnicity is more of an attachment to a group of people and set of customs.

➤ Puerto Rican ethnicity includes more than a "Hispanic race" because it includes a national, territorially-based cultural identity.

VIII. Ethnic Conflict

A. Social Distance

1. *Social distance* is a measurement of how "distant" two ethnicities or social groups are from each other, but not in a spatial sense of distance.

2. Often, groups perceived as very different from the majority, or powerful, group are marginalized and targets of discrimination by the more powerful social group.

3. *Ethnocentrism* is one group's use of its cultural identity as the superior standard by which to judge others. Ethnocentrism often causes discriminatory behavior.

B. Ethnic Cleansing

1. *Ethnic cleansing* is a process in which a racial or ethnic group attempts to expel from a territory another racial or ethnic group.

2. *Genocide* is the killing of a racial or ethnic group by another racial or ethnic group.

➤ Slobodan Milosevic, the Serb leader of the former Yugoslavia, led a genocide campaign against ethnic Albanians living in Kosovo, a region of Serbia.

IX. Gender

A. Gender

1. *Gender* is another category of classifying humans reflecting not just biological, but also social differences between men and women.

2. Social concepts of what is "masculine" and what is "feminine" vary across space and time.

B. Gender Gap

1. The *gender gap* refers to the differences in social, economic, and political power and opportunity between men and women.

C. Patterns Related to the Gender Gap

1. High *maternal mortality rates*, or death rates among women giving birth, indicate that women in poorer regions are 100 to 600 times more likely to die giving birth than are women in wealthier countries.

2. High *female infanticide rates*, or the murder of female infants, exist in regions where families want male children to carry on the family name or be able to earn more money for the family. Policies such as China's one-child policy can cause higher female infanticide rates.

3. A *dowry death* occurs when a bride is murdered by her husband's family because her father failed to pay her dowry, or marriage money. Dowry deaths in India were rising in the 1980s, but have been declining.

4. Women were not given the right to vote, called *enfranchisement,* until the 20th century in most places.

5. *Gender imbalances* also exist in places like India and China, where men outnumber women. This has contributed to higher rates of male depression as a result of men's inability to find female mates, which has, in turn, contributed to higher rates of prostitution, drug use, and HIV infection.

6. There are gender empowerment indexes that measure the degree of balance between male and female equity in society. These measurements are often used in assessing a country's level of development: the more parity between men and women, the higher the level of the country's development.

X. Folk and Popular Culture

A. Folk Culture

1. *Folk culture* is limited to a smaller region and a smaller group of people than popular culture.

2. Folk cultures are usually isolated groups that have had long-lasting culture traits that have not changed substantially over long periods.

   ➤ An example of folk culture is the Amish use of horse-drawn carriages in their communities instead of the popular culture trait of using cars.

3. Folk culture often spreads through relocation diffusion, when the original group moves to another location and takes their folk traits with them.

B. Popular Culture

1. *Popular culture* (pop culture) is mass culture that diffuses rapidly.

2. Often, folk cultures either have not been exposed to popular culture or they have chosen not to adopt popular culture.

3. Popular culture often spreads through expansion diffusion across space and varied cultures.

4. Some people believe the diffusion of popular culture is threatening local or regional distinctiveness and causing *cultural homogeneity,* or cultural sameness.

   ➤ The spread of Starbucks is argued to be reducing the diversity of local coffee shops throughout the country.

> The spread of Western media, English language usage, and Western foods is often seen as threatening non-Western cultural distinctiveness.

5. The spread of popular culture is also seen by many to be harming the environment as many popular culture traits lead to increased consumption of Earth's limited natural resources and waste production.

> Landfills are stockpiled with plastic water bottles, a fad that has recently developed to replace drinking tap water.

C. Cultural Imperialism

1. The diffusion of popular culture can contribute to cultural conflict, when part of a culture group may protest the arrival of a type of popular culture in its region.

2. *Cultural imperialism* is the invasion of a culture into another with the intent of dominating the invaded culture politically, economically, and/or socially.

3. *Cultural nationalism* is the resistance by a group of people against cultural imperialism and cultural convergence. Nationalists who believe McDonald's is a symbol of American cultural imperialism have attacked McDonald's restaurants in regions of Europe, Asia, and Africa.

4. Globalization is often seen as causing cultural imperialism and the controversy surrounding its cultural consequences.

D. Maladaptive Diffusion

1. Popular culture does not necessarily reflect its original environment, or point of invention.

2. *Maladaptive diffusion* is the adoption of a diffusing trait that is impractical for a region or culture.

> Wearing blue jeans is a popular culture trait that has diffused across space and cultures. But people wear blue jeans even in warm months, even though blue jeans originated more as winter clothing.

> The rise of fast-food consumption and car usage in Pacific Island nations where these are very expensive, unnecessary, and impractical is another example.

Religion

I. Understanding Religion

A. Defining It

1. *Religion*, a fundamental part of human culture, is a set of beliefs and activities that often help humans celebrate and understand their place in the world.

2. Religion can have a profound effect on human interaction with their environment and other cultures, thereby shaping the development of a people's cultural landscape.

B. Universalizing vs. Ethnic Religions

1. *Universalizing religions* try to have a universal appeal and attract all people to their beliefs. Christianity, Islam, and Buddhism are examples of universalizing religions.

2. About 60 percent of the world's people follow a universalizing religion.

3. Universalizing religions can often be broken into branches, denominations, and sects.

   i. *Branches* are large, fundamental divisions in a religion.

   ii. *Denominations* are groups of common congregations within a branch.

   iii. *Sects* are smaller groups that have broken away from a recognized denomination within a branch.

4. *Ethnic religions* attempt to appeal not to all people but to only one group, perhaps in one place or of one ethnicity. Judaism and Hinduism are examples of ethnic religions.

C. Monotheistic vs. Polytheistic Religions

1. Religions that believe in one supreme being are considered *monotheistic*. Christianity, Islam, and Judaism are examples of monotheistic religions.

2. Religions that believe in more than one supreme being are considered *polytheistic*. Some have argued in the past that Hinduism is polytheistic because worshippers have thousands of deities. However, many Hindus argue that they believe in one supreme being but that their religion has many deities representing different facets of the one god.

Test Tip

The AP Human Geography exam focuses more on how religion impacts elements of the cultural landscape. Focus your studies on how aspects of a religion impact the way people interact with each other and Earth, rather than specific beliefs of a religion.

II. Buddhism

A. Origins of Buddhism

1. Buddhism was the world's first universalizing religion, founded in India near the *Indo-Gangetic Hearth*, which is the area between the Indus and Ganges rivers.

2. It was founded by *Prince Siddhartha Guatama (Buddha)*, who was born in 644 BCE (before common era).

B. Diffusion of Buddhism

1. After spreading throughout India, Buddhism next spread to China, Korea, Japan, Tibet, Mongolia, and Southeast Asia along the Silk Road.

2. Buddhism is now almost extinct in India, where it was founded.

3. Nearly 350 million people worldwide are Buddhist.

C. Primary Branches of Buddhism

1. Buddhism's primary branches are Theravada and Mahayana Buddhism, but Lamaism in Tibet can also be considered a branch of Buddhism.

2. *Theravada Buddhism* is monastic, meaning all its followers are monks and nuns. It is practiced by nearly 55 percent of all Buddhists, mainly in Southeast Asia.

3. *Mahayana Buddhists* do not spend time as monks, but find salvation through meditation and prayer. It is practiced by nearly 40 percent of Buddhists, mainly in Korea, Vietnam, Japan, and China.

4. *Lamaism* in Tibet (now a region in China) combines the monasticism of Theravada with local images of deities and demons. It is practiced by about 5 percent of all Buddhists. The Chinese government has been blamed for trying to suppress Lamaism and has exiled their chief leader, the *Dalai Lama.*

D. Cultural Landscape Features

1. Buddhism's most famous structure is the *pagoda,* which is derived from ancient burial mound shapes. According to Buddhist tradition, Buddha reached enlightenment under the *Bodhi tree* in India, which is the site of many pilgrimages.

III. Christianity

A. Origins of Christianity

1. Christianity was the second universalizing religion to develop and began about 600 years after Buddhism as an offshoot of Judaism.

2. It originated in the *Semitic Hearth,* which is near modern-day Israel, when its prophet, *Jesus Christ,* was seen as the expected messiah by disciples.

B. Diffusion of Christianity

1. Christianity diffused primarily through expansion and relocation diffusion from its hearth in Palestine.

2. Christianity currently has the largest number of world adherents, with about 2 billion followers.

3. The spread of Christianity was widened and accelerated in 312 CE (common era) when the Roman Empire adopted Christianity as its official religion.

4. Moreover, when Europeans expanded their colonial efforts in the 15th century, they carried Christianity with them.

5. Different forms of Christianity have diffused to new parts of the world. For example, evangelicalism has diffused to parts of the Caribbean and Brazil.

C. Primary Branches of Christianity

1. Its primary branches are Roman Catholic, Protestant, and Eastern Orthodox.

2. *Roman Catholics* make up the largest and original piece of Christianity, with nearly 830 million adherents. It is considered a hierarchical religion because of its well-defined governance structure, with the pope at its helm.

   ➤ There are no prominent divisions or denominations within the Roman Catholic branch of Christianity.

   ➤ The Roman Catholic Church's headquarters is in Vatican City, an autonomous region in Italy.

3. *Protestant Christians* make up about 25 percent of all Christians. The Protestant branch is broken into denominations, of which the Baptist, Methodist, Pentecostal, and Lutheran are the largest.

   ➤ Protestantism has its origins in the Reformation, which occurred in the 15th century.

4. *Eastern Orthodox Christianity* developed in 1054 CE, when the Roman Catholic Church split. It is a collection of self-governing churches, the largest of which is the Russian Orthodox Church.

> The Eastern Orthodox branch of Christianity is dominant in Eastern Europe and Russia. It has its roots in Constantinople, modern-day Istanbul.

D. Cultural Landscape Features of Christianity

1. Christianity is a monotheistic religion with a main holy book called the *Bible.*

2. The varied nature of Christian-influenced cultural landscapes reflects the changes that have occurred in the religion throughout its history.

3. Prominent cathedrals in the cityscape tower above feudal villages as symbols of the leading influence that the Roman Catholic Church was in medieval life.

4. Defiantly simple, wooden, plain churches define Protestant communities and outposts in what was the "New World," a haven for Protestants from England before the Revolutionary War.

5. Baroque cathedrals with ornate sculptures and domes were constructed by Catholics trying to combat the Reformation movement in 17th-century Europe.

6. Christians also use up the most land of all religions for burial, whereas Hindus, Buddhists, and Shintoists cremate their dead.

   > Class differences are also evident in burial grounds where gravestones of wealthier Christians are often more prominent than poorer adherents.

IV. Islam

A. Origins of Islam

1. Islam was the third major universalizing religion to develop; it originated in Mecca, Saudi Arabia, around 600 CE through its prophet, *Muhammad* (sometimes spelled Mohammed).

B. Diffusion of Islam

1. Muhammad carried Islam to Media, Saudi Arabia, from where it diffused globally.

2. With nearly 1.2 billion adherents, it is the second-largest religion. It is also the fastest-growing religion.

3. Islam's successful diffusion led to the Crusades, which were efforts by Christians in the 11th and 12th centuries to "take back" and "save" lands from the diffusing Muslims. Today, such a competition between Islam and Christianity continues in some parts of the world, especially in areas of Africa.

4. In the era of globalization, Islam is also a substantial part of European and North American cultures.

C. Primary Branches of Islam

1. Though some Muslims believe there are no branches in Islam, many see that there are two primary braches of Islam, Sunni and Shiite.

2. *Sunni Muslims* (Sunni means "orthodox") account for about 85 percent of Muslims. Sunnis dominate in the Arabic-speaking areas of Bangladesh and Pakistan.

3. *Shiite Muslims* are the majority in Iran and Iraq, though Sunnis controlled the government of Iraq under former President Saddam Hussein.

   ➤ Shiites account for nearly 15 percent of all Muslims and believe more strictly that only direct descendents of Muhammad should rule Islam.

D. Cultural Landscape Features of Islam

1. Islam is a monotheistic religion with a holy book called the *Koran.*

2. The most prominent feature of Islamic cultural landscape is the mosque, or center of Muslim worship. It is often the center of a Muslim town's focus and often has four minarets, or towers used to call worshippers.

3. Islam's prohibition of depicting human form in architecture is the primary reason so many mosques are ornately designed with geometric patterns.

4. One of the *Five Pillars of Islam*, which are somewhat analogous to the Ten Commandments of Christians and Jews, requires most Muslims to make a *pilgrimage* (or religious journey) to *Mecca*, the holiest site to Muslims, where Muhammad was born.

5. The second holiest site to Muslims is *Medina*, where Muslims believe Muhammad moved after receiving his knowledge of Islam.

6. The third holiest site to Muslims is the *Dome of the Rock* in Jerusalem, where Muslims believe Muhammad received his divine inspiration from *Allah* or God.

V. Sikhism

A. Origins of Sikhism

1. Sikhism is one of the smaller universalizing religions.

2. Sikhism was founded in the late 15th century in present-day Pakistan and follows the teachings of *Guru Nanak*, its chief religious prophet.

B. Diffusion of Sikhism

1. Sikhism diffused outward from its origin in Pakistan, particularly towards northern India.

2. Sikhs have a global diaspora today and are especially prominent in the U.S., Canada, the UK, former British colonies of East Africa, and Australia.

C. Cultural Landscape Features of Sikhism

1. Sikhism is a monotheistic religion and its holy book, the *Guru Granth Sahib*, contains the teachings of all of its prophets, called gurus.

2. A high concentration of Sikhs exists in the *Punjab region*, which straddles northwestern India and northern Pakistan.

3. The Punjab region is also home to Sikhism's holiest site, the *Golden Temple.*

4. In India, there are continuing tensions between Sikhs and Hindus, as some Sikhs have pushed to secede from India and form their own country.

5. Some consider Sikhism to be a *syncretic religion*, or a blend of beliefs and practices of both Hinduism and Islam.

VI. Hinduism

A. Origins of Hinduism

1. Hinduism claims more than 900 million adherents, with most living in India. It evolved in the Indo-Gangetic Hearth in about 2000 BCE, before Buddhism.

2. Hinduism is considered an ethnic religion because of its close identity with its Indian origins.

B. Diffusion of Hinduism

1. Hinduism spread from its Indo-Gangetic Hearth eastward via the Ganges and south through India.

2. Hinduism also spread to Sri Lanka and to a lesser extent the British possessions during the era of colonial rule. Hindus are also prominent in the UK, the U.S., and Canada, in addition to parts of East Africa, such as Uganda.

C. Primary Branches of Hinduism

1. There are no formal branches in Hinduism, although among its believers there are definite variations in practices.

2. Hinduism is believed to be a polytheistic religion by some but a monotheistic religion by others. Some Hindus argue that there is only one supernatural being reflected in Hinduism's many deities.

D. Cultural Landscape Features of Hinduism

1. Instead of one holy book, Hinduism has a collection of ancient scriptures called *Vedas*.

2. One of Hinduism's principal beliefs is reincarnation, or the rebirth of souls from one generation of life to another.

3. Alongside reincarnation is Hinduism's connection to India's tradition of a *caste system*, or a social hierarchy, into which people are born.

   ➤ According to the caste system, some people are born into power.

   ➤ In recent years, India's caste system has been lessening in influence because of political pressure.

4. Perhaps the most famous Hindu was *Mahatma Gandhi*, who worked to help free India from England's colonial rule in the 20th century.

5. Because Hindus believe temple builders receive divine reward, the Hindu landscape is dotted with countless shrines and temples to Hindu gods, often adorned by food offerings from believers.

6. Hindus believe in cremating their dead, so corpses are sometimes found burning alongside streets or beside rivers in Hindu areas.

7. It is considered holy to bathe in the *Ganges River* in India, so many Hindus make a pilgrimage to the river's banks to bathe.

VII. Judaism

A. Origins of Judaism

1. Judaism is the oldest monotheistic religion in the world. It originated around 2000 BCE in the *Semitic hearth* (modern day Palestine).

2. Judaism grew out of the belief system of a tribe in Southwest Asia known as the Jews, whose headquarters became Jerusalem.

3. The roots of the faith exist in the teachings of Abraham, who, interestingly, is connected to Christianity's prophet, Jesus Christ, who considered himself a Jew.

B. Diffusion of Judaism

1. After the Roman Empire destroyed their holy city of Jerusalem, the Jews scattered throughout the world, known as the Jewish *diaspora* (the scattering of an ethnic group).

2. The Jews moved into central Europe and towards the Iberian Peninsula.

3. Many Jews now live in Israel, the only country in which Judaism is not a minority religion.

4. Israel was declared the official Jewish homeland in 1948, a declaration that triggered a war with its Arab neighbors.

5. The largest population of Jews is found in the U.S., but Judaism is also prominent in major cities of western Europe.

C. Primary Branches of Judaism

1. *Orthodox Judaism* seeks to retain the original teachings of the faith.

2. *Reform Judaism* developed in the 1800s as a branch attempting to adjust the religion to fit more modern times.

3. *Conservative Judaism* is the most recent of the branches and is more moderate in its approach to religion than either Reform or Orthodox.

D. Cultural Landscape Features of Judaism

1. Judaism's holiest teachings are contained in the *Torah,* which consists of Old Testament teachings and the Talmud, the collection of rabbinical and historical teachings passed down from one generation to the next.

2. Perhaps the most prominent feature in the Jewish-influenced cultural landscape is the *synagogue,* or Jewish house of worship and community gathering. Though architecturally varied, all synagogues have an ark housing their sacred book, the Torah, written in Hebrew.

3. An important symbol in Judaism is the six-pointed star.

4. Perhaps the holiest site to Jews is Jerusalem's Western Wall, which is believed by Jews to be the westernmost remaining side of the Temple Mount complex, which once housed two Jewish holy temples destroyed by invaders.

5. Many Jews try to make pilgrimages to the Temple Mount to see the Western Wall and offer prayers and mourn the destruction of their holy temples.

6. Importantly, the Muslims' holy Dome of the Rock is only feet from the Jews' holy Western Wall.

   ➤ This intersection of sacred sites in Jerusalem's cultural landscape has led to centuries-long conflict over control of this sacred space.

VIII. East Asian Ethnic Religions

A. Shintoism

1. *Shintoism* is a syncretic, ethnic religion blending principles of Buddhism with a local religion of Japan.

2. From the 1800s until after World War II, Shintoism was the state religion of Japan.

B. Taoism (or Daoism) and Confucianism

1. Taoism is linked to the philosopher *Laozi*, who lived around the 6th century BCE, the same time as *Confucius*, another philosopher.

2. In his writings, Laozi taught that people should live in harmony with nature and all aspects of their lives. This created *feng shui*, the practice of organizing living spaces in harmonious ways.

3. Confucius built a system of morals and a way of life for Chinese in areas such as government, religion, education, and philosophy. Confucianism focuses more on the worldly life rather than the ideas of heaven and hell.

4. Both Taoism and Confucianism have spread beyond China to the Korean Peninsula, Japan, Southeast Asia, North America, and Europe. There has been some conflict between China's Communist government and religions.

IX. Shamanism and Animism

A. Shamanism and Animism

1. *Shamanism* is a term given to any ethnic religion in which a community follows its shaman, or religious leader, healer, or truth knower.

2. Shamanism has its strongest presence in Africa, but has historically existed in North America, Southeast Asia, and East Asia. Shamans are also still important in the Amazon and in parts of Mexico and Guatemala.

3. Some shamans teach *animism*, a belief that objects such as trees, mountains, and rivers have divine spirits in them. Native American religious beliefs often have animistic traits, finding spiritual and religious signifiance in features of the landscape.

X. Secularism and Theocracy

A. Secularism

1. Secularism is the movement away from control of life by a religion. Secularists are often associated with being indifferent to religion or rejecting it all together. Many Western democracies have secular principles, formally declaring the separation of government and religion.

B. Theocracy

1. *Theocracy*, on the other hand, is a government run by a religion.

   ➤ For example, a theocracy existed in the former government of Afghanistan, in which the Taliban, a group of fundamentalist Muslims, controlled all aspects of life for the Afghani people. Currently, Iran is another modern example of a theocracy.

XI. Interfaith vs. Intrafaith Boundaries

Place	Interfaith Boundary	Conflict
China (Tibet)	Tibetan Buddhism and Atheism	The atheist Chinese government is allegedly destroying Tibetan Buddhist monasteries and arresting and exiling its adherents to suppress religion in the area and assimilate the region to Chinese control.
Nigeria	Islam and Christianity	Islam prevails in the northern region, while Christianity and local religions prevail in the south. Such division causes power-based tensions for control of the one government.
India	Hinduism and Sikhism	Sikhs in the northwestern state of Punjab demand autonomy from the Hindu-controlled government of India.
India and Pakistan	Hinduism and Islam	Pakistan, once a part of India, was established in 1947 as a Muslim state. Pakistan and India are conflicting over control of the northern territory known as Jammu and Kashmir.
Former Yugoslavia	Christianity and Islam	In the Yugoslavian civil wars of the 1990s, Serb leader Slobodan Milosevic (an Eastern Orthodox Christian) tried to kill or evict the Muslim population in Bosnia and other Serb-controlled lands in the region.

Place	Intrafaith Boundary	Conflict
Palestine (modern-day Israel)	Judaism and Islam	For centuries, Jews and Muslims have fought for control of Palestine. This fight intensified after the creation of Israel following World War II.
Iraq	Sunni Islam and Shiite Islam	After the fall of the largely Sunni government controlled by Saddam Hussein, both Sunnis and Shiites are warring for control of the newly forming political landscape.
United States	Christian fundamentalism and moderate, liberal Christianity	Christians have conflicted not just in the U.S. but also worldwide over political-cultural issues such as homosexuality, evolution, and abortion. In some cases, violent tactics have been used.
Northern Ireland	Protestant Christians and Roman Catholics	British colonialism deposited large numbers of Protestants in traditionally Catholic Northern Ireland. This intrafaith boundary has caused violent conflicts between the two groups in the region.

A. Interfaith vs. Intrafaith Boundaries

   1. *Interfaith boundaries* divide space between two or more religions whereas *intrafaith boundaries* divide space within one religion, often among denominations.

B. Examples of Interfaith Boundaries

   1. China (Tibet): Tibetan Buddhism vs. Atheism

      ➤ The atheist Chinese government is allegedly destroying Tibetan Buddhist monasteries and arresting and exiling its adherents to suppress religion in the area and assimilate the region to Chinese control.

2. Nigeria: Islam and Christianity

➤ Islam prevails in the northern region of Nigeria, while Christianity and local religions prevail in the south.

➤ Such division causes power-based tensions for control of the one government.

3. India: Hinduism and Sikhism

➤ Sikhs in the northwestern state of Punjab demand autonomy from the Hindu-controlled government of India.

4. India and Pakistan: Hinduism and Islam

➤ Pakistan, once part of India, was established in 1947 as a Muslim state.

➤ Pakistan and India have been conflicting over control of the northern territory known as Jammu and Kashmir.

5. Former Yugoslavia: Christianity and Islam

➤ In the Yugoslavian civil wars of the 1990s, Serb leader Slobodan Milosevic (an Eastern Orthodox Christian) tried to kill or evict the Muslim population in Bosnia and other Serb-controlled lands in the region.

6. Palestine (including modern-day Israel): Judaism and Islam

➤ For centuries, Jews and Muslims have warred for control of Palestine.

➤ This fight intensified after the creation of Israel, following World War II.

C. Examples of Intrafaith Boundaries

1. Iraq: Sunni Islam and Shiite Islam

➤ After the fall of the largely Sunni government controlled by Saddam Hussein, both Sunnis and Shiites are warring for control of the newly-forming political landscape.

2. United States: Christian Fundamentalism and liberal Christianity

➤ Christians have conflicted not just in the U.S., but also worldwide over political-cultural issues such as evolution and abortion. In some cases, violent tactics have been used.

3. Northern Ireland: Protestant Christians and Roman Catholics

➤ British colonialism deposited large numbers of Protestants in traditionally Catholic Northern Ireland.

➤ This intrafaith boundary has caused violent conflicts between the two groups in the region.

Language

I. Language Evolution

A. Proto-Tongue

1. Language is a culture trait, learned from one generation to another.

2. It is speculated that nearly 2.5 million years ago, language first developed in order to organize human activity.

3. All original speakers communicated in the *proto-tongue*, or original language.

4. Once speakers diffused to various places on the Earth through migration, language divergence occurred and new languages and dialects spawned from the proto-tongue.

B. Language Divergence

1. *Language divergence* occurs when speakers of the same language scatter and develop variations of that original form of the language to meet their needs in the new surroundings.

   ➤ The proto-language may not have had words for concepts such as "snake" or "iceberg." Once the human group came into contact with these new concepts, they created new words for them.

C. Language Shift

1. When speakers come into contact with other languages, a blending of the two or more languages can occur.

2. *Language replacement* occurs when invaders replace the language of those places they conquer.

3. Language replacement can lead to *language extinction,* when a language is no longer used. Some argue that Latin is facing language extinction, as fewer and fewer people are using Latin.

D. Reverse Reconstruction

1. Geographers can trace diffusion paths of language through *reverse reconstruction,* the process of tracking a language's diffusion.

2. The process begins with the most recent places of the language's existence and moves backward through time, comparing words with geographic places and groups of people using the same or similar words.

➤ For example: *If* two languages share a common word for an extinct animal *and* that animal only existed in one of the many places where the two languages are now spoken, *then* one possible conclusion is that the language diffused from the place where the extinct animal once existed and the speakers carried with them the word for the hearth's extinct animal.

II. The Language Tree

A. Organization of the Language Tree

1. Linguists have organized languages into a language tree.

2. The tree is subdivided into the following hierarchy

➤ 19 language families

➤ Each family has its own branches

➤ Each branch has its own groups

➤ Each group has its own language

➤ Each language has its own dialects

B. Some Major Language Families

Language Family	Approximate Number of Languages	Percentage of World's Speakers	Approximate Number of Speakers (in millions)
Indo-European	430	44.78%	5,960 (5.9 billion)
Sino-Tibetan	399	22.28%	1,275 (1.2 billion)
Niger-Congo	1,495	6.26%	358
Afro-Asiatic	353	5.93%	339
Austronesian	1,246	5.45%	311
Dravidian	73	3.87%	221

(Source: ethnologue.com)

C. Top 10 *Native* Languages

Language	Speakers
Mandarin Chinese	885,000,000
Spanish	332,000,000
English	322,000,000
Bengali	189,000,000
Hindi	182,000,000
Portuguese	170,000,000
Russian	170,000,000
Japanese	125,000,000
German (Standard)	98,000,000
Wu Chinese	77,175,000

(Source: ethnologue.com)

Test Tip

As with religion, focus your studies on spatial patterns associated with different languages, rather than memorizing facts about individual languages. For success on the AP exam, it is much more important to think about where different languages exist, how they have diffused, and how language is a factor in power, conflict, and human-environment interaction.

III. **The Indo-European Family**

A. General Facts

1. About 50 percent of all people speak an Indo-European language, most prominently English.

2. English is part of the Germanic branch of the Indo-European language family.

3. Other major branches of the Indo-European language family include the Balto-Slavic, Romance, and Indo-Iranian branches.

B. Proto-Indo-European

1. The original Indo-European language is referred to as *Proto-Indo-European.*

2. New languages developed through language diversification as a result of migration of Proto-Indo-European speakers from the hearth of this language family.

3. The location of the hearth of the Proto-Indo-European language is the subject of speculation.

4. Because modern Indo-European languages share words for "snow" but not "sea," the hearth is believed to have been somewhere with snow, but distant from the sea.

5. Linguists estimate its origin to have been between 6000 and 4500 BCE.

6. As the Proto-Indo-European speakers diffused by using horses and the wheel, the language evolved into various forms.

C. Conquest Theory of Indo-European Diffusion

1. The *conquest theory* argues that Indo-European diffusion began in the empire-building Kurgan culture located in the steppe region of Russia, north of the Caspian Sea.

D. Agriculture Theory of Indo-European Diffusion

    1. The *agriculture theory* argues that Indo-European diffusion started in a farming community in Europe's Danube River region.

IV. **Language-Related Conflict**

A. Multilingual States

    1. *Multilingual states* are countries in which more than one language is spoken.

    2. Multilingual states often contain *linguistic minorities*, or groups of speakers who are outnumbered by speakers of another language in the country.

    3. When there are power imbalances among linguistic groups, this can lead to conflict over language and its ties to national identity and power.

B. Monolingual States

    1. *Monolingual states* contain speakers of only one language.

    2. Because of the increasing pace of spatial-cultural interaction globally, purely monolingual countries no longer exist. One might argue, however, that Japan is relatively monolingual with its stringent immigration laws.

    3. Countries like France have fought to preserve their monolingual heritage. For example, French politicians have called for laws to keep French pure and prohibit the infusion of English words into their vocabulary.

C. Some Conflicts Related to Multilingualism

    1. The following table lists some recent conflicts related to multilingualism. Keep in mind that the conflicts highlighted in the table reflect multifaceted conflicts, not singularly related to language. Instead, language is an important symbol of the ethno-cultural divisions at the root of the conflict in these regions.

Place	Languages	Conflict
Canada	English and French	French speakers, concentrated in Quebec, have fought for increased recognition and power against the English-speaking Canadian majority. Some Quebec citizens have even called for secession from Canada.
Belgium	Dutch and French	The Dutch-speaking north and French-speaking south compete for power and control. The nation's capital city, Brussels, is located in the Dutch-speaking south, but most inhabitants are French speakers.
Cyprus	Greek and Turkish	The Greek majority and Turkish minority compete for control of this island-country. Cyprus is divided by a "Green-Line" partition separating the two cultures.
Nigeria	Hausa, Yoruba, Ibo and nearly 230 other languages	Hausa speakers in the north, Yoruba in the southwest, and Ibo in the southeast paint a divided Nigeria in which some 230 other languages complicate Nigeria's unification. English was declared the official language as an attempt to create a tool of common communication.

 V. **Official and Standard Languages**

A. Official Language

1. An *official language* is declared by the leaders of a country to be the language used in legal and governmental proceedings. Countries or regions often declare an "official" language to define and declare national identities.

2. An official language is often the language of the powerful, linguistic majority.

> In 2006, the U.S. engaged in a national debate surrounding the longstanding call by some Americans for a declaration that English be the official language of the United States.

3. Declaration of an official language is often controversial.

> In Nigeria, English was chosen as a neutral choice, rather than one of the three largest languages in the country, to prevent calls of dominance by one group over another.

> In Sri Lanka, one part of the civil war was about declaring Sinhala the official language and not giving status to Tamil.

B. Standard Language

1. *Standard language* is the acceptable form of a given language as declared by political or societal leaders.

> The British government declared *British Received Pronunciation (BRP)* English as the standard form of the language to be taught in all schools, rather than American English.

> German schools teach High German (Hoch Deutsch), a form of German originally spoken by the powerful aristocrats in the upper Rhine region of Germany.

 VI. **Language and Imperialism**

A. *Lingua Franca*

1. A *lingua franca* is a language used to facilitate trade among groups speaking different languages.

2. In the multilingual region of East Africa, hundreds of native languages are spoken but people turn to Swahili as their *lingua franca* to communicate with speakers of other languages when they need to trade or conduct business.

3. The *lingua franca* in a region is often rooted in colonialism and imperialism, such as the use of French in Cameroon and Sengal and English in India.

B. Pidgin Language

1. When regions are invaded or economically dominated by a foreign-language speaking group, the dominated group is often forced to pick up the language of the dominators in order to trade with them and conduct business.

2. When the dominated culture picks up the new language, they usually speak a *pidgin,* or simplified version, of the dominators' language.

   ➤ When the French dominated the Caribbean region, the native people began speaking a pidginized (simplified) form of French.

C. Creolization

1. Once a pidginized language becomes part of a culture and is written down, it becomes known as a *creole* (or creolized) language, or a pidgin language that has become the main language of a group of people.

   ➤ In the Caribbean, pidgin French became such a part of life that it became the mother language of the dominated people, thus becoming a creole.

VII. Place Names

A. Toponyms

1. *Toponyms* are place names that reflect cultural identity and impact the cultural landscape.

2. People take great pride in naming their place, which can become a controversial task because determining a toponym can indicate ownership and control over space.

   ➤ Controversy erupted in India when the government announced it would rename the city of Bombay to rid the place of its English colonizers' toponym (Bombay). The new toponym, Mumbai, angered some Muslims because it relates to a Hindu god.

3. Toponyms can also give clues into origins and aspirations of their related cultures.

   ➤ Saint Petersburg, Russia, was named by Czar Peter the Great, perhaps conveniently after his patron saint, Peter.

   ➤ Santa Barbara, California, reflects both the Spanish-Portuguese language and Catholic influences, as "Santa Barbara" is Spanish for Saint Barbara, a Catholic martyr.

   ➤ Consider what these toponyms indicate about the people and cultures who named these places: Paradise, California; Hope, Arkansas; and Hell, Michigan!

Political Organization
of Space

I. Territory

A. Defining Political Geography

1. *Political geography* is the study of human political organization of the Earth at various geographic levels.

2. Scholars study political geography at three scales: the supranational scale, the national/country scale, and the sub-national (or local) scale.

3. Above the country scale, political geographers study organizations such as the United Nations, which includes many countries.

4. At the country scale, political geographers look at how a country's government is organized.

5. Below the country scale, political geographers might study the boundaries of voting districts, for example.

6. Political geographers also study the changing role of the country in the world's political affairs.

B. Human Territoriality

1. *Territoriality* is creating ownership over a defined space.

2. Territoriality can apply to your bedroom or an entire country and often evokes an emotional response.

   ➤ Consider when Iraq invaded Kuwait's territory and triggered the first Gulf War or when Germany invaded Poland in 1939, causing England and France to come to Poland's defense.

C. Personal Space

1. Territoriality also applies to the geography of personal space.

2. *Personal space* is the area we claim as our own territory into which others may not enter without our permission.

   ➤ A student sitting at a classroom desk, for example, may claim that her personal space extends around her desk, like a bubble.

3. How much space is considered "personal" often varies with time and place.

   ➤ People living in small towns often have larger "bubbles" of personal space than do, for example, New Yorkers, who deal with crowded subways and streets.

D. Sovereignty

1. *Sovereignty* is the internationally recognized control a place has over the people and territory within its boundaries.

   ➤ Germany, Russia, Japan, Indonesia, the United States, and Vietnam are just a few of the nearly 200 countries on Earth with sovereignty.

   ➤ The sovereignty of Taiwan has been disputed by China, as was the sovereignty of Kurdistan by Iraq under Saddam Hussein's regime.

II. **States and Nations**

Political geography has been a favorite topic tested in the AP exam free-response questions. Be sure to think carefully through states, nations, and political conflicts related to various centripetal and centrifugal forces. Be sure to have a few good examples tucked away to use if asked such a question.

A. States

1. Political geographers use the term *state* to refer to countries.

2. In political geography, then, a *state* is a political unit with a permanent population, territorial boundaries that are recognized by other states, an effective government, a working economy, and sovereignty.

B. Nations

1. Political geographers use the term *nation* to refer to a group of people who share a common culture and identify as a cohesive group.

2. Language, religion, a shared history, and territory are cultural elements that can create such cohesion and form a nation.

3. Internal differences often exist within a people who consider themselves nations. The sense of belonging together as a nation can, however, override these differences.

   ➤ Different Native American nations, such as the Cherokee and Chickasaw, have internally unique traits, though Native Americans often feel a sense of belongingness to a broader, Native American nation.

4. People are often willing to fight on behalf of their national identity.

5. Conflict occurring between different nations is referred to as *ethnonational* conflict.

C. Multinational States vs. Nation-States

1. A *multinational state* is a state (or country) that includes more than one nation within its borders.

   ➤ The Soviet Union was a multinational state that contained hundreds of nations within its borders, such as the Chechens, Belarusians, Udmurts, and Ukrainians, to name just a few.

2. A state with only one nation in its borders is called a *nation-state*.

> ➤ Japan and Iceland are examples of states that are the closest in today's world to be considered nation-states.

D. Brief History of the Nation-State Concept

1. Humans have organized political space in different forms throughout their existence.

2. Early humans organized into clans, tribes, and villages. When, in the course of history, these small groups were conquered, they were combined to form kingdoms and empires.

3. The ancient Greeks and Romans refined a component in their empires by creating the *city-state*, in which political space revolved around a central city and surrounding farmland.

4. After the fall of the Romans around 500 CE, European territory was divided into a non-centralized, feudal structure, loosely based on grouping territories by religion.

5. In about the 1500s, many Western European places began integrating these feudal structures into more centralized kingdoms.

6. The loosely organized, feudal state began to fade away in England and France as a strong monarchy emerged.

7. With the stronger monarchy came more internal cohesion in the political organization, which led to the rise of *nation-states*, a more cohesive group of people linked to their territory through a shared government and common goals.

8. This pattern of integration into nation-states diffused throughout Europe and became a common goal through World War II.

9. The idea of linking people who share a strong sense of unity (a nation) under one government seemed to be the best way to prevent ethnonational violence from erupting, as it did in both of the world wars.

E. Stateless nations

    1. When a nation does not have a territory to call its own, it is referred to as a *stateless nation.*

    ➤ The Assyrian Christians of Iraq, the Kurds in the Middle East, and the Ughirs of western China do not have their own states and, as such, are considered stateless nations.

III. Ethnonationalism and Conflict

A. Ethnonationalism

    1. *Ethnonationalism* is a powerful emotional attachment to one's nation that occurs when a minority nation within a state feels different from the rest of the state's people.

    2. When a minority feels that they do not have enough *self-determination*, or the power to control their own territory and destiny, ethnonationalism can lead to conflict.

    ➤ The Chechen people comprise a minority nation that live in Russia and have a strong sense of ethnonationalism that has led to violent conflict with the Russian government.

B. Irredentism

    1. Members of a nation do not always live in just one place.

    ➤ The Serbs are a nation, but they exist in several countries, not just the land that is considered Serbia.

    2. Conflict can arise when a nation's homeland is spread into the territory of another state or several states.

    3. *Irredentism* is a movement by a nation to reunite its parts when they have spread across other borders.

    ➤ An example of irredentism occurred when Hitler believed that the German nation had spread into Czechoslovakian territory, he wanted to take control of that land in Czechoslovakia to reunite Germans into one state.

Some Recent Conflicts Related to Ethnonationalism

Place	Conflicting Parties	Reason
South Asia, Indian subcontinent	India and Pakistan	These two parties are fighting over control of Kashmir, a region overlapping each country's sovereignty and homelands.
Palestine, Southwest Asia	Jewish Israelis versus Muslim Palestinians and Arab allies	The stateless nation of Muslim Palestinians and their Arab allies are warring against the Jewish-controlled state of Israel for autonomy in a deeply-layered, historical conflict.
Southeast Asia	Mainland China and Taiwan	Taiwan was founded in the 1940s after non-Communists fled the Communist government established on mainland China. China does not recognize Taiwan as a sovereign state and sees Taiwan as an island belonging to it, although Taiwan feels it is independent of China and is its own democratic state.
Former Yugoslavia	Serbs versus all the other nationalities that were once part of "Yugoslavia"	The former Yugoslavia comprised many nations, including Serbs, Croats, Kosovar Albanians, and Bosnian Muslims. In the 1990s, different nations in the multinational state of Yugoslavia warred to break away from the Serb-dominated government in Belgrade. Several newly independent states were created as a result of this war, the bloodiest since World War II.
Russia	Russia versus Chechnya	Chechnya is a State in the Russian republic, governed by Moscow. The Chechen people want independence from Russia, which has caused fighting between the two groups.

C. Buffer States and Zones

1. A *buffer state* is an independent country located between two larger countries that are in conflict.

   ➤ Russia and China have warred over boundaries for centuries, but Mongolia, a buffer, has helped reduce direct confrontation between the two states.

   ➤ Afghanistan was considered a buffer state between Russian and British imperial interests.

2. A *buffer zone* exists when two or more countries sit between two larger countries in conflict.

   ➤ After World War II, Eastern Europe was a buffer zone between the Soviet Union and Western Europe.

D. Satellite States

1. *Satellite states* are countries controlled by another, more powerful state.

2. During the Cold War, the Soviet Union worked to dominate the Eastern European buffer zone and install Communist satellite states there.

   ➤ Poland became a satellite state of the Soviet Union, controlled by Moscow.

3. The installation of Communist satellite states in Eastern Europe formed what Winston Churchill called an "iron curtain" boundary between Western Europe and Soviet-controlled Eastern Europe.

E. Shatterbelts

1. A *shatterbelt* is a state or group of states that exists within a sphere of competition between larger states and is often culturally, economically, and politically fragmented and splintered.

   ➤ Eastern Europe is often referred to as a shatterbelt, as it existed as a sphere of competition between the USSR and Western powers and was culturally, economically, and politically fragmented.

2. Often, states in a shatterbelt are the victims of invasion, boundary changes, and poor economic development.

IV. Boundaries

A. Types of Political Boundaries

1. *Geometric political boundaries* are straight-line boundaries that do not relate to the cultural or physical features of the territories involved.

   ➤ The original boundaries separating North and South Korea followed a line of latitude.

2. *Physical (or natural) political boundaries* separate territory according to natural features in the landscape, such as mountains, deserts, or rivers.

   ➤ France is divided from Spain by the Pyrenees Mountains.

3. *Cultural political boundaries* mark changes in the cultural landscape, such as boundaries that divide territories according to religion or language. Sometimes cultural political boundaries are drawn according to geometric straight lines.

   ➤ The borders that carved modern-day Pakistan were created to give Muslims a territory.

B. Frontiers

1. *Frontiers* are regions where boundaries are very thinly or weakly developed, zones where territoriality is unclear and not well established.

   ➤ Antarctica is a frontier region because it does not have clear boundaries of territorial control.

   ➤ Saudi Arabia and Yemen have a frontier boundary.

2. Local communities can have frontier regions between neighborhood boundaries.

3. Boundaries are lines; frontiers are regions.

C. Boundary Evolution

1. Another way to classify boundaries depends not just on how they were created, but on how they have evolved over time.

2. *Antecedent boundaries* existed before human cultures developed into their current forms.

   ➤ Many physical political boundaries grew as antecedent boundaries.

   ➤ Kentucky and Indiana grew as distinct cultures around an already present divider, the Ohio River.

3. *Subsequent boundaries* grow to divide space as a result of human interaction and negotiation after significant settlement has occurred.

   ➤ The division between Canada and the United States is an example of a subsequent boundary because the boundary developed because of settlement patterns and related negotiations.

4. *Superimposed boundaries* are forcibly put on the landscape by outside parties, such as invaders or an organization such as the United Nations.

   ➤ The boundary creating the modern state of Israel was superimposed by the United Nations.

5. A *relict boundary* no longer functions as a boundary, but only as a reminder of a line that once divided space.

   ➤ Perhaps one of the most famous relict boundaries is the Berlin Wall, which no longer serves as an administrative border as it once did in dividing East and West Berlin.

D. Boundary Creation

1. There are several steps on the growth of boundaries into final form.

2. *Definition* is the phase in which the exact location of a boundary is legally described and negotiated.

3. *Delimitation* is the step when the boundary's definition is drawn onto a map.

4. *Demarcation* is the visible marking of a boundary on the landscape with a fence, line, sign, wall, or other means.

> ➤ Not all boundaries are demarcated because it can be an expensive process.

5. *Administration* is the enforcement by a government or people of the boundary that has been created.

E. Ocean Boundaries

1. The United Nations has led the world's efforts in creating boundaries of shared waters.

2. According to the *United Nations Convention on the Law of the Seas*:

i. Coastal states can stake their claims to the sea up to 12 nautical miles from their shorelines. However, ships from other countries have the right to pass through these waters.

ii. A coastal state can claim up to 200 nautical miles of territory beyond its shoreline as an *exclusive economic zone*, over which that state has economic control to explore and mine natural resources that may be in the waters.

iii. Where there is not enough water for each country on opposite sides of the sea to have 200 nautical miles of exclusive economic zone, the two or more countries involved will divide up the water evenly, a rule called the *median line principle*.

F. Types of Boundary Disputes

1. Conflicts over boundaries are divided into different categories, but sometimes involve a mix of the following categories:

i. *Definitional boundary disputes* are fights over the language of the border agreement in a treaty or boundary contract.

> ➤ Japan and Russia have still not agreed on the definition of territorial boundaries surrounding islands north of Japan.

ii. *Locational boundary disputes* occur when the conflicting parties agree on the definition but not on where the boundary exists on the Earth or the map.

iii. *Operational boundary disputes* are conflicts over the way a boundary should operate or function, such as if migration should be allowed across the border.

iv. *Allocational boundary disputes* are fights over resources that may not be divided by the border, such as natural gas reserves beneath the soil.

 V. **Shapes of States**

A. Territorial Morphology

1. Factors like shape, size, and relative location affect the political issues facing its people internally and internationally.

2. *Territorial morphology* is the relationship between a state's geographic shape, size, relative location, and its political situation.

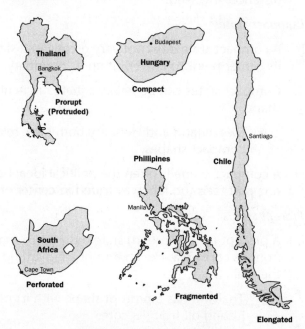

Shapes of Various States

B. Classifications of Geographic Shapes of States

1. *Fragmented states*

    i. Fragmented states geographically exist in several pieces.

        ➤ Indonesia, for example has over 16,000 islands in its fragmented nature!

        ➤ Malaysia is broken into two chunks.

    ii. A fragmented shape can lead to problems for a state to maintain unity among its constituent parts, such as in East Timor, which broke away from Indonesia.

2. *Elongated states*

    i. Elongated states are long and thin in shape.

        ➤ Vietnam and Chile both have elongated shapes.

    ii. Sometimes problems can arise with this shape when a state's power base, or capital, loses influence over one end of the elongation.

    iii. It can also pose transportation problems because of the distances involved.

3. *Compact states*

    i. A compact state does not vary greatly in distance from its center point to any point on its boundary.

    ii. Compact states can be nearly square or circular in shape.

        ➤ Switzerland and Hungary both have relatively compact shapes.

    iii. A compact shape is often the political ideal because no one part feels too far away from the center of control.

4. *Prorupt states*

    i. A prorupt (or protruded) state has a piece that protrudes from its core area, like an arm or a leg jutting off from the main body.

        ➤ Thailand has a prorupt shape with its protrusion jutting off from its core.

ii. Prorupt states often face similar problems to those felt by elongated states, as the protruding piece may try to break away or it may be invaded.

5. *Perforated states*

   i. Perforated states have a hole punched in them by another state, like South Africa, which is perforated by Lesotho, a tiny country.

   ii. In other words, a perforated state completely surrounds another state.

   iii. Relationships between the perforated state and its perforating state can be difficult and can cause tension, particularly if the perforated state is not welcoming of the perforating state's peoples.

6. *Landlocked states*

   i. Countries that are landlocked, or without coastal access to a body of water, must depend on their neighbors to get to water sources for trade and navigation.

      ➤ Lesotho is landlocked and must depend on South Africa for permission to travel to the coast and for airspace navigation.

VI. Internal Political Organization of States

A. Unitary Governmental Structure

1. A state's size and cultural composition are also factors in its political situation and internal organization.

2. States that are smaller in geographic size and population may be more politically unified, but not always.

   ➤ A *microstate* is a very small state, such as Singapore.

3. Oftentimes, these smaller, homogeneous states will organize using a *unitary governmental structure,* in which there is one main governmental decision-making body for the entire state.

4. Regions within a unitary governmental structure may have their own local governments, but they are weak and serve only as administrative organs of the unitary government based in the country's capital.

5. A unitary government can even take the form of a dictatorship.

B. Federal Governmental Structure

1. Larger, more diverse states often adopt a *federal governmental structure*, such as in the United States and Germany, where there is a central government and strong regional governments that share power with the central government.

2. The regional governments have different names; called "states" in the United States, Germany, and India; "provinces" in Canada; and "estados" in Mexico. (Note that in this case, the use of "state" refers not to a country, but to a provincial unit.)

3. Federal governmental organization is ideal for countries that may be geographically large and/or have regions that want a sense of *self-determination*, freedom from domination by the central government.

4. The United States organized into a federal structure so that each state, such as Tennessee and New Jersey, was given a sense of power and agreed to unify into one country.

5. The danger of organizing a multinational state into a federal structure is that some regions, when given autonomy, may choose to break away from the unified state and demand complete independence.

   ➤ There have been secession movements in Vermont, Alaska, and Hawaii, as people in these states have rallied around breaking away from the greater United States and forming their own country.

C. Confederation Structure

1. Another governmental organizational structure is the *confederation* (or *confederal*) *structure* in which a weak central government exists with regional governments holding the majority of power.

   ➤ The Articles of Confederation was the first document binding together the 13 American colonies, primarily for the purpose of defense during the Revolutionary War.

VII. Political Enclaves and Exclaves

A. Political Enclave

1. A territorial *enclave* is a state, or part of a state, surrounded completely by another state.

   ➤ Lesotho is an enclave territory surrounded by South Africa.

   ➤ West Berlin was an enclave within the state of East Germany.

B. Political Exclave

1. When an enclave is land that is a political extension of another state, then it is called an *exclave*.

   ➤ The West Berlin enclave in East Germany was technically a part of the West German state, making that West Berlin enclave also an *exclave* of West Germany.

   ➤ Alaska is an exclave of the United States because it is cut off from the rest of the country by Canada.

VIII. Colonialism and Imperialism

A. Colonialism

1. *Colonialism* is the control by one state over another place. Often, a state that is colonizing has a more industrialized economy than the region it is taking over.

2. European nation-states began building world empires in the 16th century and competing for territories across the globe up through World War II.

3. The first period of colonialism occurred after European explorers, such as Columbus, discovered land in the Western Hemisphere in the 15th century.

4. The second major wave occurred in the late 1800s, as western European powers were competing to "carve up" Africa, gaining more land to make them appear more powerful and to feed their industrializing economies.

   ➤ England and France occupied nearly 70 percent of colonial territory in Africa.

   ➤ Portugal, Germany, Spain, Italy, and Belgium also colonized Africa.

B. Mercantilism

1. Europeans raced to form colonies in the Western Hemisphere in order to extract resources to send back home.

2. *Mercantilism* is an economic system in which a state acquires colonies that can provide it with the raw materials to ship back home and use in making products for the population of the mother country.

3. Other motives for colonization were to spread Christianity and to bask in the glory of having more land than other states.

C. Imperialism

1. Colonization fueled *imperialism*, the process of establishing political, social, and economic dominance over a colonized area.

2. Europeans acculturated indigenous peoples to European Christianity and culture, even destroying indigenous landscapes and imposing European architecture to signify dominance.

D. Dependency Theory

1. According to the *dependency theory*, many countries are poor today because of their colonization by European powers.

2. Proponents of this theory assert that former colonies in South America, Africa and Asia have not been able to heal from the imperial domination established by the European colonizers and are still dependent upon them.

3. In most cases, the political boundaries drawn by the colonizers were drawn according to the resources available to the colonizers, not according to the cultural (national) groupings of the native people.

4. When the colonizers left and these lands became independent states, the populations in those states were not unified, which often fueled violent ethnonational conflicts, such as in Nigeria and Sudan.

5. Many colonial subjects still trade with former colonial rulers as their primary source of income, such as Senegal and France.

E. Neocolonialism (Post-Colonial Dependency)

1. The continued economic dependence of new states on their former colonial masters is called *neocolonialism* (or *post-colonial dependency*).

2. Because the political and economic structures established by the Europeans benefited the colonizers, not the local people, essential elements of infrastructure were not built in most colonized lands.

3. When the European colonizers left, education systems, health care networks, roads, communication lines, and other basic elements were not in place for the regions to thrive on their own.

4. Additionally, many former colonies were left without the finances or ability to develop these basic elements of infrastructure for their people. They were left with little choice but to turn back to their former colonizers and ask for loans in order to try to build up their economies that were, arguably, destroyed by their colonizers.

5. Even in situations in which there was no colonial relationship, disproportionate political and economic power creates an unequal relationship between two or more countries.

IX. Geopolitics

A. Geopolitics

1. *Geopolitics* is a branch of political geography that analyzes how states behave as political and territorial systems.

2. In other words, geopolitics is the study of how states interact and compete in the political landscape.

B. Organic Theory

1. Nineteenth-century geopolitical thinker Friedrich Ratzel's *organic theory* argues that states are living organisms that hunger for land and, like organisms, want to grow larger and larger through acquiring more nourishment in the form of land.

   ➤ Adolph Hitler and the Nazis used Ratzel's theory to justify invading other states in order to feed the German state's organic hunger for land.

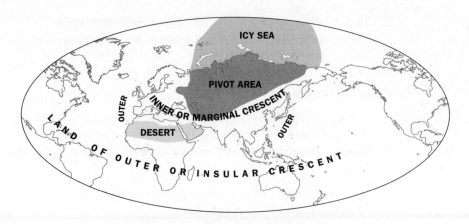

Mackinder Heartland Theory

C. Heartland Theory

1. According to Halford Mackinder's *heartland theory*, the era of sea power was ending and control over land would be the key to power.

2. Mackinder believed that Eurasia was the *world island* and the key to dominating the world. Ruling the world necessitated controlling Eastern Europe.

3. Mackinder's theory is linked to the Communists' efforts to dominate Eastern Europe and to the United States' "containment policy" of keeping the Russians from gaining additional territories in the heartland.

D. The Domino Theory

1. The *domino theory*, prevalent during the Cold War, warns that the democratic allies must protect lands from falling to the Communists because one such Communist acquisition creates others, ultimately resulting in Communist domination of the world (like falling dominos).

2. The domino theory led to the containment doctrine, intended to keep the Communists from acquiring new lands, such as Vietnam.

E. Rimland Theory

1. In his *rimland theory*, geopolitical thinker Nicolas Spkyman built on Mackinder's theory and defined the *rimland* to be Eurasia's entire periphery, not its core of Russia and Central Asia.

2. Spkyman's rimland encompassed Western Europe, and Southeast, South, and East Asia.

3. Spkyman thought it was important to balance power in the rimland to prevent a global power from emerging.

4. The rimland theory is linked to the Vietnam and Korean wars, in which Communists and non-Communists fought for control of peripheral lands in the rimland.

X. Challenges to Inherited Political-Territorial Arrangements

A. Core and Multicore States

1. The region in a state wherein political and economic power is concentrated, like the nucleus of a cell, is called a state's *core*.

2. A well-integrated core, one that functions as a healthy part of its state, not in isolation, helps spread development throughout the country.

3. Countries having more than one core region are called *multicore states*.

4. In a multicore state where there is not one dominant core, internal divisiveness can occur when different core areas compete for political and economic power.

   ➤ Nigeria has several core regions competing for control and jeopardizing Nigeria's unification.

5. Strong infrastructural development, in the form of roads, communication lines, and so forth, can help distribute the growth generated in a core to less developed areas in a state.

B. Primate Cities

1. Some countries have a capital city, called a *primate city*, that is not only the political nucleus but is also more economically powerful than any other city in the state.

2. Primate cities often exist in less developed countries, where most of the resources are attracted, like a magnet, to one city that grows and grows and is supplied by the smaller cities in the state that do not get an equal share of the development.

   ➤ Ulaanbatar, Mongolia, is an example of a primate city that is many times larger and more powerful than the next largest city in Mongolia.

   ➤ Lagos, Nigeria, is another example of a primate city that is many times larger and more powerful than the next largest city in Nigeria.

3. In countries with primate cities, governments often try to spread the growth and development out among different cities, rather than just allowing it to focus on the primate city.

4. Primate cities are also common in old nation-states, like France and Britain. In these places, the primate city has been the cultural center for a long time and still attracts many migrants.

C. Forward Capitals

1. A *forward capital* is a capital city built by a state in order to achieve some national goal.

   ➤ The Russian czar Peter the Great built the forward capital city of Saint Petersburg, moving the capital of Russia from Moscow, to bring Russia's capital city and its focus closer to Europe.

> Islamabad, Pakistan, is a forward capital. Constructed in 1960, it was specifically built to spread development out more evenly across Pakistan and to position Pakistan's government in a more strategic geographic position than Karachi, its former capital.

> Brasilia, Brazil, is also a forward capital, constructed to move Brazil's capital from the coast to a geographically interior position in the country.

D. Gerrymandering

1. Redrawing electoral boundaries to give a political party an advantage is called *gerrymandering*.

2. The definition of these boundaries can give one party an advantage over another in competing for a spot in a legislature.

> For example, boundaries can be drawn to give the number of registered Republicans a majority in a particular district, or registered Democrats a majority in another district.

3. The spatial organization of electoral geography can have a profound effect on power structures in a state.

E. Centrifugal and Centripetal Forces

1. Within every state are forces that unify its regions and people, and there are forces that work to divide its regions and people.

2. *Centrifugal forces* divide and tear apart a state's people and regions.

> Centrifugal forces broke apart the former Soviet Union, leading to independent states such as Latvia, Lithuania, and Estonia, which were once part of the Russian union.

3. *Centripetal forces* unify a state's people and regions.

4. In states that are unified, centripetal forces are more dominant than centrifugal forces. On the other hand,

centrifugal forces are more dominant when a state is breaking apart.

5. *Balkanization* occurs when centrifugal forces break apart a state into smaller pieces.

Test Tip

To remember the difference between centrifugal and centripetal forces think:

Centrifugal = "F" for "fracture"

Centripetal = "T" for "together"

Some Examples of Centripetal and Centrifugal Forces within States*

Centrifugal	Centripetal
Separatism in a region	Unifying symbols, such as flags
Internal boundary conflicts	A national pledge of allegiance
Deep religious divisions	A strong identity based on language, religion, or other cultural traits

F. Devolution

1. *Devolution* is the process of transferring some power from the central government to regional governments.

   ➤ Devolution often refers to the transfer of power that occurs when a state breaks up, when regions that were once unified in one, central government gain power and, sometimes, independence.

2. States facing centrifugal forces, such as strong regional separatism or internal dispute, are often forced to transfer

---

* These examples could be reclassified depending on the situation. A flag, for example, might be a unifying, centripetal factor in the United States of America, but a force of division and conflict in a state that cannot agree on what the flag should look like. A culture trait such as religion can also help strengthen national ties or weaken them.

power to regional governments to reduce the divisive tensions by giving angry groups more regional power and autonomy.

➤ Scotland was pushing for more autonomy from England. In the 1990s, England devolved more power to Scotland, when Scotland was given its own representative parliament instead of only being governed by England's parliament in London.

XI. Supranationalism

A. Supranationalism

1. *Supranationalism* is the growing trend to organize political and economic affairs at the international level rather than the national level. Supranational organizations refer to entities in which three or more countries form an alliance for cultural, economic, or military reasons.

2. Supernatural alliances are created so that states can collectively reach a common goal that they may not be able to reach independently.

3. If a country threatens other states, the affected supranational organizations may impose *international sanctions*, or punishments in the form of economic and/or diplomatic limits or even isolation.

➤ When Iraq was threatening members of the United Nations, the UN imposed economic sanctions on Iraq, including trade embargoes—complete bans on trade with Iraq.

4. The growth of supranational alliances challenges conceptions of state sovereignty. To join such an alliance, states must often give up some powers they have to the organization.

➤ Some European countries were reluctant to give up their currencies and convert to the European Union's currency, the euro. Notably, the United Kingdom has thus far decided not to convert to the euro.

B. Some Examples of Supranational Organizations

1. After the bloody conflict among states during World War I, U.S. President Woodrow Wilson, along with other world leaders, founded the League of Nations, though the U.S. did not join.

2. After World War II, countries came together and formed the United Nations for collective security to try to ensure that a global war (such as WWII) would not again be allowed to happen.

3. With nearly 200 members, the United Nations is the world's most extensive supranational organization ever established.

4. During the Cold War, the Warsaw Pact was a supranational organization of Communist allies, while the North Atlantic Treaty Organization (NATO) was formed to combat the expansion of Communist states.

5. The Association of Southeast Asian Nations (ASEAN), another example of political supranationalism, was formed in the 1960s to protect its member states from invasion by China.

C. The European Union

1. *Economic supranationalism* is the integration of three or more states for achieving collective economic goals.

2. The European Union (EU) is an example of economic supranationalism and represents the growth of a European economic community that has been formally developing since the 1950s.

3. Historically, the EU started to grow with the formation of the Benelux, an economic alliance among Belgium, the Netherlands, and Luxembourg before the end of World War II.

4. Through Benelux, these three countries benefited from reduced trade barriers, more easily crossable (or permeable) borders, and common goals.

5. Other European countries learned from this idea, and in 1958, the European Economic Community (also called the Common Market) was formed among some states wanting economic integration and cooperation.

6. Out of the Common Market developed an even larger grouping of states, the European Community, with hopes of becoming more than just an economic union.

7. By 1992, the European Union (EU) was formed with economic, political, cultural and judicial integration goals.

8. The EU member states have bound together their economies, currencies, and environmental policies to create a powerful internal market in Europe.

9. Most member countries use the euro, a common currency.

10. Some geographers think that the EU will soon evolve into a military alliance as well among member states.

D. A New World Order

1. During the Cold War, in the aftermath of World War II, states were divided into two camps, pro-Communist and pro-democracy.

2. World power in such a bi-polar world (dominated by two powers) was relatively balanced by this division. A geopolitical transition has occurred since the fall of the Soviet Empire in the 1990s.

3. In this new world order after the Cold War, international relations are no longer driven by the bi-polar Communist/ anti-Communist groups.

4. Economically, many superpowers dominate the market, including the U.S. economy, the European Union, and the growing Chinese economy.

5. Militarily, the United States maintains superpower status, but is increasingly challenged by terrorism and other types of warfare.

Agriculture and Rural Land Use

I. Development and Diffusion of Agriculture

A. Defining Agriculture

1. Most people practice *agriculture,* the growing of plants or raising of animals, in order to produce food for sustenance for sale at the marketplace.

2. Prior to the domestication of plants, humans were primarily nomadic hunters and gatherers, unable to settle in one place for too long before they had to move on to new food resources.

3. Today, farms provide humans with the ability to stay stationary and build cities. Less than 250,000 people in the world are hunters and gatherers.

B. Subsistence versus Commercial Farming

1. Despite the widespread adoption of agriculture, there are substantial differences in the way developed and less developed countries farm.

2. *Subsistence farming* is when a farmer can grow only enough food to feed his/her own family. In many less developed regions of the world, people are subsistence farmers.

3. *Commercial farming* is when farmers grow food to be sold in groceries and markets, not just to be eaten by the farmers themselves. In the more developed countries, like the United States, most farms are commercial farms. Worldwide, commercial farming is increasing as subsistence farms are being incorporated into the global farming market.

C. Origins of Agriculture

1. Geographers generally believe that humans evolved from hunters and gatherers into stationary farmers over thousands of years, as humans constantly touched and handled plants in their gathering efforts to feed themselves.

2. Geographers believe that agricultural innovation occurred in and diffused from multiple *hearths,* or places of origin.

3. According to Carl Sauer, humans first learned how to grow plants in Southeast Asia through *vegetative planting,* a process of simply cutting off a stem of another plant or by dividing up roots of a plant.

   ➤ Southeast Asia has a climate and terrain that would have supported the growth of root plants that are easily divided, such as the taro, yam, banana, and palm.

4. From the *Southeast Asian hearth,* this knowledge diffused north and east to China and to Japan, and then west towards Southwest Asia, Africa, and the Mediterranean region.

5. Other early vegetative hearths are believed to have emerged through independent innovation in northwestern South America, near the Andes Mountains, and in West Africa.

6. Later, humans made the leap in the First Agricultural Revolution to *seed agriculture,* which is farming through planting seeds, rather than simply planting part of the parent plant. Seed agriculture leads to higher crop yields, since there are so many seeds.

D. The First Agricultural Revolution

1. The *First Agricultural Revolution* (or *Neolithic Revolution*) saw the human development of seed agriculture and the use of animals in the farming process about 12,000 years ago.

2. The growth of seed crops, like wheat and rice, and the use of animals, such as goats and sheep, replaced the hunting and gathering nomadic lifestyle that had existed since humanity was born.

3. Human groups were able to stay in one place, grow their populations, and start to build communities.

4. The ability to produce more food without roaming for it increased the carrying capacity of the Earth, which charted the path towards the development of civilization.

5. Like the advent of vegetative planting, the First Agricultural Revolution is believed to have occurred *independently* in several hearths.

Seed Agricultural Hearths

Hearth	Diffusion Route	Crop Innovation
Western India	To Southwest Asia	Wheat and barley
Southwest Asia (near Tigris and Euphrates rivers)	To Europe (first in Mediterranean regions like Greece and then north through Danube River); North Africa; and to northwestern India and Indus River area	Integrated seed agriculture with domestication of herd animals such as sheep, cattle, and goats, which helped in the farming process
Northern China	To South Asia and Southeast Asia	Millet (a small yellow grain)
Ethiopia	Remained isolated in Ethiopia	Millet (or rather an even smaller millet-like grain known as teff)
Southern Mexico	Throughout Western Hemisphere	Squash and corn
Northern Peru	Throughout Western Hemisphere	Squash, cotton, beans

E. The Second Agricultural Revolution

1. After the fall of Rome around 500 CE, farming grew into a feudal village structure.

2. During the Middle Ages, most farmers worked their lands to feed themselves and their families in an *open-lot system*, one in which there was one large plot of community farmland that all villagers farmed to produce a crop to eat.

3. As capitalism grew, feudalism diminished and villages enclosed their farmland.

   ➤ The *enclosure movement* gave individual farmers their own plots of farmland, marking a major shift in agriculture.

4. Geographers still debate where and when the Second Agricultural Revolution began, although nearly all agree its most influential phase coincided with the Industrial Revolution in 17th- and 18th-century England and Western Europe.

5. The growing industrial economy and the decline of feudal villages in the 1600s and 1700s caused massive urban migration, as former farmers moved into cities in England and Western Europe for work.

   ➤ This wave in urban migration caused a great jump in the demand for food to be shipped into cities for the workers.

6. With this demand came new innovations in farming and transportation technology that dramatically increased crop and livestock yields.

   ➤ New agrarian (farming) technology was invented, such as a better collar for oxen and the use of the horse instead of the ox on the farm.

   ➤ New fertilizers, field drainage and irrigation systems, and storage systems were invented to help increase farm outputs.

7. Higher farm outputs also encouraged the population boom that accompanied the Industrial Revolution.

 II. Types of Subsistence Farming

A. Shifting Cultivation

1. In *shifting cultivation,* subsistence farmers rotate the fields they cultivate (or farm) in order to allow the soil to replenish its nutrients, rather than farming the same plot of land over and over.

2. Shifting cultivation is different from *crop rotation*, in which the farmer changes the crop-type, not the plot of land, in order to keep the soil healthy.

> ➤ Farming the same type of crop repeatedly on the same plot of land leaches the soil of nutrients that are needed for healthy crops.

3. Shifting cultivation is often found in the tropical zones, especially rain forest regions in Africa, the Amazon River basin in South America, and throughout Southeast Asia because the topsoil is thin in these regions, making it necessary to change the plot of land frequently to grow healthy crops.

> ➤ The primary cause of poor soil quality in these regions is the heavy tropical rains that wash away soil nutrients.

B. Slash-and-Burn Subsistence Farming

1. The common way that farmers in these regions prepare a new plot of land for farming is through *slash-and-burn agriculture,* a form of subsistence agriculture in which the land is cleared by cutting (or slashing) the existing plants on the land, then burning the rest to create a cleared plot of new farmland (called *swidden*).

2. The slash-and-burn method is a form of *extensive subsistence agriculture,* using a large amount of land to farm food for the farmer's family to eat.

3. Slash-and-burn (swidden) is not dependent on advanced technology, only on human labor and the presence of extensive acreage because plots are frequently abandoned once the soil quality becomes poor and new land must be made swidden for a new crop.

4. Often swidden farmers will mix different seeds on the same plot of farmland, a practice known as *intertillage.*

> ➤ Intertillage helps grow food for a balanced diet and reduces the risk of crop failure.

5. The slash-and-burn method has caused environmental problems in some areas.

➤ Because of rising population pressures, farmers need to produce more food for more people on less land.

➤ Many swidden agriculturists are being forced to reduce the period of time the farmed land lies *fallow,* the period the farmland is not farmed and recuperates from producing a crop.

➤ By farming it too fast, the soils are damaged and never fully regain their nutrients.

6. Shifting cultivation is being replaced by more money-making farming practices, like cattle-ranching, logging, and production of cash crops to sell in the global marketplace.

➤ Instead of the rotating, regenerative methods of shifting cultivation, more destructive forms are being used, such as permanent clearing of the rain forests by commercial farming companies.

C. Intensive Subsistence Farming

1. *Intensive subsistence agriculture* is when a farmer cultivates a small amount of land very efficiently to produce food for the farmer's family to eat.

➤ Intensive subsistence agriculture is usually found in fertile areas that are highly populated, such as China, India, and Southeast Asia.

2. Remember, subsistence farming is not intended for sale at the marketplace; its intent is *not* farming surpluses for sale but is, instead, producing enough food for the farming family to survive.

3. *Extensive subsistence agriculture* is intended for low population densities with extensive amounts of available land.

4. Intensive subsistence farmers make the most use of their small plots of land to feed their families, often showing ingenuity in their techniques, such as the terrace-farming "pyramids" often seen in the Southeast Asian farming landscapes.

5. Rice is the dominant intensive subsistence agriculture crop in areas such as South China, India, Southeast Asia, and Bangladesh where summer rainfall is abundant.

6. In areas with winters that are too cold for rice, grains such as wheat, corn, and millet are grown on intensive subsistence farms.

7. Often, intensive subsistence farmers will practice *double-cropping*, planting and harvesting a crop on a field more than once a year.

   ➤ Growing corn in one season and wheat in another is one example of double-cropping.

D. Pastoralism

1. *Pastoralism* is a form of subsistence agriculture involving the breeding and herding of animals to produce food, shelter, and clothing for survival.

2. Pastoralism is usually practiced in climates with very limited, if any, arable land, such as grasslands, deserts, and steppes.

3. Sometimes, pastoralism can be sedentary, when pastoralists live in one place and herd their animals in nearby pastures; or it can be nomadic, when the pastoralists travel with their herds and do not settle in one place for very long.

   ➤ Nomadism has been an important part of Mongolian agriculture and history.

4. Often pastoralism involves the herding of cattle, sheep, camels, and goats and is practiced in arid climates in North Africa, central and southern Africa, the Middle East, and central Asia.

5. Nomadic pastoralists often practice *transhumance*, the movement of animal herds to cooler highland areas in the summer to warmer, lowland areas in the winter.

6. Like other forms of subsistence agriculture, pastoralism is declining worldwide, as governments work to use dry lands for other purposes, like oil drilling in the Middle East.

➤ Pastoral nomads are being confined to less and less land and encouraged to incorporate themselves into the global farming economy.

III. Mediterranean Agriculture

1. *Mediterranean agriculture* is primarily associated with the region near the Mediterranean Sea and places with climates that have hot, dry summers and mild, wet winters.

   ➤ California, Chile, southern South Africa, and South Australia are places where Mediterranean agriculture is found.

2. Mediterranean farming involves wheat, barley, vine and tree crops, and grazing for sheep and goats.

   ➤ Olives, grapes, and figs are staple tree crops on Mediterranean farms.

3. Mediterranean agriculture can be either extensive or intensive, depending on the crop.

   ➤ While wheat is farmed extensively, olives are intensively farmed.

4. Mediterranean farming is both subsistence and commercial, depending on where it is practiced.

IV. Commercial Farming

A. Defining Commercial Farming

1. *Commercial farming* is different from subsistence farming in that commercial farmers produce their crops to sell them in the marketplace.

2. Commercial farming types include mixed crop and livestock farming, ranching, dairying, and large-scale grain production.

3. Plantation farming is a form of commercial farming, but it is practiced mostly in less developed countries.

B. Mixed Crop and Livestock Farming

1. *Mixed (crop and livestock) farming* involves a farm that grows crops and raises animals.

2. Most of the crops grown on mixed farms are used to feed the farm's animals, which in turn provide manure fertilizer as well as goods for sale, such as eggs.

3. Most of a mixed farm's income comes from the sale of its animal products. This reduces a mixed crop and livestock farmer's complete dependence on seasonal harvests because the animal products are not as dependent on the season as the crops are.

4. Mixed farming exists widely throughout Europe and eastern North America, usually near large, urban areas with limited land available for more extensive practices.

5. Most mixed farms practice crop rotation in which the field is subdivided into different regions, each region growing a different seed and rotating over time. Crop rotation allows the nutrients of the soils to replenish, as each seed leaches different nutrients from the soil.

C. Ranching

1. *Ranching* is commercial grazing, or the raising of animals on a plot of land on which they graze.

2. Ranching is usually extensive, requiring large amounts of land.

3. Since meat and wool are products that are highly demanded, cattle and sheep are the most common animals on ranches.

4. Ranching is practiced in areas where the climate is too dry to support crops, but it is declining in importance.

➤ Ranching is most practiced in the western United States, Argentina, southern Brazil, and Uruguay. Ranching is rare in Europe, except for Spain and Portugal.

➤ Many former United States ranches are being converted into "fattening" farms on which fixed-lot cattle are fattened before being slaughtered to feed the explosive growth in the beef industry.

➤ Ranching is quite common also in the tropical deciduous forest regions on the west coast of Latin America and northern Mexico.

5. The decline of ranching is partially caused by low grain prices and partially by a system of meat quality standards in the U.S. that values fat meat over lean meat.

➤ Latin American beef is grass-fed, lean, and tough.

D. Dairying

1. *Dairying* is the growth of milk-based products for the marketplace.

2. Dairy farms closest to the marketplace usually produce the most perishable, fluid-milk products, while those farther away produce goods such as cheese and butter.

3. It is the most economically productive type of commercial agriculture practiced near cities in the northeastern United States, southeastern Canada, and northwestern Europe.

4. Farms are usually very small and capital intensive.

➤ *Capital-intensive farms* use a lot of machinery in the farming process, whereas *labor-intensive farms* use more human labor.

5. The *milkshed* is the zone around the city's center in which milk can be produced and shipped to the marketplace without spoiling.

6. The growth in transportation technology, such as refrigerated trucks, has enabled dairy farmers to locate farther from the city's center, thus increasing the area of the milkshed. In fact, improved technology and feeding systems have led to increases in the amount of milk produced per cow.

E. Large-Scale Grain Production

1. Wheat is the dominant grain on *large-scale grain farms,* where the grains are most often grown to be exported to other places for consumption.

2. Large-scale grain production is most common in Canada, the United States, Argentina, Australia, France, England, and the Ukraine (which was once considered the "breadbasket" of Russia), although the United States is the world's largest large-scale grain producer.

3. Wheat is the world's leading export crop and is dominated by U.S. and Canadian farms, which grow collectively over half of the world's wheat.

   ➤ Many grain farms produce grain to be consumed by the animals farmers plan to sell or eat later.

   ➤ Much of the land in Western Europe devoted to grain farming is simply producing grain for animal feed.

4. Large-scale grain farms grew during the Industrial Revolution, creating large city-based populations needing wheat and other grains for consumption.

5. Large-scale grain farms are usually highly mechanized, capital-intensive operations.

6. Several technological innovations precipitated the growth of large-scale grain farming:

   ➤ The *McCormick Reaper,* developed in the 1830s, is a machine that cuts standing grain in the field.

   ➤ The *Combine Machine* completes all three processes of reaping, threshing, and cleaning in one machine.

F. Plantation Farming

1. *Plantation agriculture* involves large-scale farming operations, known as plantations or agricultural estates, that specialize in the farming of one or two high-demand crops for export, usually to more developed regions.

2. Plantation agriculture was introduced in tropical and subtropical zones by European colonizers who were seeking to produce crops such as coffee, tea, pineapples, palms, coconuts, rubber, tobacco, sugar cane, and cotton.

   ➤ Cotton was particularly important in the southern U.S. as an export crop produced on plantations by black Africans who were kidnapped and forced into slavery schemes.

3. Today, plantation agriculture is still largely reflective of global power structures. Most plantations exist in low-latitude regions of Africa, Asia, and Latin America but are owned by companies (or individuals) from more developed countries who often take some of the best farmland from native farmers, leaving local farmers with little land.

4. Most plantations exist in a location that has easy coastal access for exporting their crops to be sold in foreign markets.

5. Though modern plantations have integrated advanced technology into their farming practices, plantation agriculture is still labor-intensive and require the hiring of large numbers of seasonal workers during harvest times.

   ➤ A form of plantation agriculture remains in the subtropical and tropical United States, where migrant workers are used for labor.

   ➤ Hawaii has its own plantations, but there is a strong growers' union and the products are, therefore, more expensive.

V. Von Thünen Agricultural Location Theory

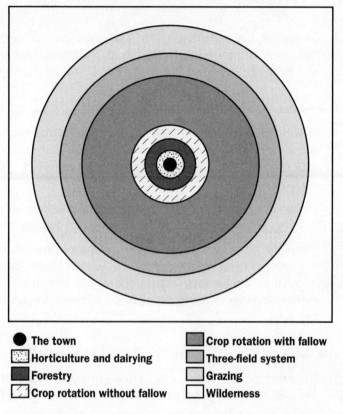

Legend:

- ● The town
- ▦ Horticulture and dairying
- ■ Forestry
- ▨ Crop rotation without fallow
- ▩ Crop rotation with fallow
- ▢ Three-field system
- ▢ Grazing
- ☐ Wilderness

Von Thünen's Model of Agricultural Land Use

A. Basic Parts of the Model

1. *Johann Heinrich von Thünen* was a 19th-century German economist who formulated a model explaining and predicting where and why different agricultural activities would take place around a city's marketplace.

2. Von Thünen began by establishing several assumptions on which to build his model.

   ➤ He assumed there is only one city with one, central marketplace where all farmers sell their products and try to make the most money they can.

> ➤ He assumed that the farmland is all equally farmable and productive and there is only one type of transportation mode.

3. Given these assumptions, von Thünen allowed for only one variable to change in his model: *the distance a farm's location was from the city's market as evident in transportation costs.*

B. The Agricultural Settlement Pattern Predicted by the Model

1. In von Thünen's model, the central marketplace is surrounded by agricultural activity zones that are in concentric rings. Each ring represents a different type of agricultural land use.

2. Moving outward from the city's central marketplace, the farming activities changed from intensive to more extensive.

3. Inversely, if you were to travel from the outermost rings into the city's central marketplace, you would travel through rings of extensive farming practices, like grazing, into more intensive farming practices, such as horticulture and dairying.

C. The Reasons Explaining the Von Thünen Model's Predictions

1. The land closest to the city's marketplace is more expensive per unit than is land farther away from the city's center.

2. A grain farmer who needs a lot of land for his/her extensive farming operation is going to purchase a farm farther from the city's marketplace because the land is *less* expensive.

3. A milk producer is likely to buy land closer to the city's center because he/she doesn't need the extensive land a grain-farmer needs to produce the same profit.

> ➤ Additionally, the dairy farm needs to be closer to the marketplace so milk can be quickly transported to the marketplace for sale before it spoils.

4. Grazing is often the land use farthest outward from the city's marketplace in the ring with the lowest "land rent" because grazing requires so much land and makes the least amount of money per unit of land.

D. Usefulness of Von Thünen's Model

1. Von Thünen's model is useful in comparing real situations to his *theoretical* farming situation, one that is restricted to one thing changing (called "the variable")—transportation costs.

2. In the real world, agricultural land use patterns depend on more than one variable.

3. Von Thünen knew his work was based on his theoretical assumptions, so he introduced some variations, such as the existence of a river running through the city, the possibility of multiple marketplaces, and the idea that soil was not of equal quality everywhere in the model.

4. Overall, the model emphasizes the influence of distance as a factor in human location decisions.

   ➤ According to von Thünen, farming decisions, like so many other spatial patterns, relate to distance.

   ➤ Geographers analyze farming land uses in particular areas and compare them to von Thünen's hypothetical situation in order to explain what they see and predict future land-use patterns.

VI. **Settlement Patterns In Villages**

Housing Building Materials

Material	Regions Commonly Found
Wood	Eurasia, U.S. Pacific Coast, North America, Australia, Brazil and Chile
Stone	Europe, Egypt, India, western China, Yucatan, Mexico, South-Central Africa, Middle East
Grass and brush	Low-latitude regions: African savanna, East African highlands, upland South Africa, South American highlands, Amazon Basin; northern Australia
Poles and sticks (wattle)	Africa, Southeast Asia, West Africa, Amazon Basin in South America
Sun-dried brick (more traditional; note that brick is often used where wood is not as available)	Middle East, Middle and South America, northern China, African savanna, and North Africa
Oven-baked brick	Modern, contemporary areas in more-developed countries

A. Shapes of Villages

1. Historically, the shape of a village's spatial layout was related to its function and its environment.

2. In Europe, villages were often clustered on the hillside to leave the flatlands for farming and to offer its people protection by being on an incline.

3. Many earlier villages were walled to keep invaders out.

4. In lowland areas with rivers and streams, villages were often linear in shape, following the water source, with the farmlands radiating from the linear village.

5. Other villages in Europe, Asia, and Africa were round with a space in the middle for the cattle.

6. Many villages were built according to a grid-plan with geometric boundaries.

 VII. Modern Commercial Agriculture

A. The Third Agricultural Revolution

1. The *Third Agricultural Revolution* began in 19th-century North America and saw the globalization of industrialized agriculture and new technologies that increased the food supply.

   ➤ Remember, the First Agricultural Revolution ushered in the growth of stationary plant and animal domestication and the second agricultural revolution saw new farming and storage capabilities increase food supplies to meet and facilitate a growing, industrializing population.

3. The Third Agricultural Revolution distributed mechanized farming technology and chemical fertilizers on a global level.

4. During the Third Agricultural Revolution, farming and food processing were completed at different sites.

B. The Industrialization of the Farming Process

1. After the Third Agricultural Revolution, it became increasingly common for commercial farmers to harvest their crops and ship them off to food processing sites to be packaged for marketing and distribution.

2. Similar to a factory in which different parts of the production process are completed by different departments before the finished product gets to market for sale, food-production increasingly became "industrialized."

➤ Purity Dairies in Nashville, Tennessee, provides a strong example of this industrialization in agriculture. Today, this large agricultural corporation subcontracts with local farms to buy unprocessed milk that is shipped to the Purity Dairies factory in Nashville, near the market. At the city-based factory, the milk is processed, packaged, and put on trucks for distribution within the *milkshed*. The milk-farm itself is only one component in this multi-layered, agricultural process.

C. Agribusiness

1. *Agribusiness* is the combination of the pieces of the food-production industry, including the farms, processing plants, packagers, fertilizer laboratories, distributors, and advertising agencies.

2. Agribusiness is the modern system of food production involving everything from the development of seeds to the marketing and sale of food products at the market.

3. While the percentage of farmers in the U.S. workforce has markedly declined, the number of workers involved in some way in agribusiness shows that food production is still an integral part of the U.S. and global economy.

➤ A graphic designer drawing the images for a child's prepackaged lunchbox is part of the increasingly complex agribusiness system.

➤ In 1950, about 12% of the U.S. workers were farmers. Today, less than 1% of U.S. workers claim farming as their occupation.

4. Just as a computer production process often involves an *international division of labor*—with computer chips being produced in Asia, assembled in Europe, and sold in the United States—the farming process has become divided on a global level.

➤ Many local flower farms in the United States have closed down because of the globalization of industrial agriculture; these local farmers cannot compete with corporate-owned flower farms in foreign lands that grow and ship flowers to the U.S.

Be sure to STOP and THINK about what an FRQ is "getting at" before you think you are stumped. On a past exam, an FRQ asked students about the distribution of poultry (chicken) farms in the United States. Many students felt stumped by what they thought was a highly specific question. However, students who stopped and thought through the question realized that they could gain some points by relating the pattern in chicken farms to the increase in corporate-owned farms and the decline of family farmers in the U.S. agribusiness system. More often than not, if you stop and think about the question, you will see it is asking about something more familiar to you than originally thought.

D. The Green Revolution

1. The *Green Revolution* began in the 1940s and was a phase of the Third Agricultural Revolution in which new strains of hybrid seeds and fertilizers were invented that dramatically increased the crop output.

2. The Green Revolution began with agricultural experiments that were funded by U.S. charities to find ways to improve Mexico's wheat grain production capabilities to reduce hunger in that region.

3. Scientists soon found new hybrid strains of wheat, maize, and rice that were *higher-yielding*, capable of producing more food at a faster pace.

4. Scientists also developed new fertilizers and pesticides that supported the higher-yielding seeds that required special nitrogen-enriching fertilizers and increased protection from diseases and pest infestations.

5. Green Revolution scientist *Norman Borlaug* won a Nobel Peace Prize in 1970 for his work to increase world peace through spreading hunger-reducing technology to poorer regions of the world.

6. The "miracle" of the green revolution was in its global diffusion of higher-yielding varieties of wheat, rice, and maize crops. Farmers were simply able to grow more food per unit area of farmland at a faster pace.

   ➤ Globally, grain production increased by 45 percent between 1945 and 1990.

   ➤ Asia was able to increase its rice production by 66 percent by 1985.

   ➤ India was able to supply its own wheat and rice by the 1980s.

7. Hunger and famine were reduced, but not eliminated, through the diffusion of green revolution technology. The inability to eliminate hunger is because of social and transportation problems, not a lack of food.

E. Economic Downsides to the Green Revolution

1. Green Revolution technologies have reduced the amount of human labor needed on the farm in some areas, which has cut many jobs.

2. The higher-yielding crop strains are often more prone to viruses and pest infestations, leading to higher levels of crop failure in some areas.

3. Many of the higher-yielding Green Revolution crops, such as rice and wheat, are not farmable in dryer African regions, where millet and sorghum are grown.

   ➤ Research on more African-appropriate crops has not kept pace.

   ➤ Less than 5 percent of African farmers use Green Revolution seeds.

4. Some analysts argue that the Green Revolution has increased economic inequality in peripheral countries.

> ➤ Local farmers in peripheral countries often have a
> difficult time purchasing the more-expensive green
> revolution seeds and technologies, often driving them
> out of the market and causing them economic ruin.

F. Environmental Downsides to the Green Revolution

1. Green Revolution pesticides have arguably caused pollution
   and soil-contamination problems because they drain
   through the ecosystems in which they are used.

2. Workers who are frequently exposed to these chemicals
   have suffered health problems from poisoning.

3. Because Green Revolution crops often require more
   watering, water resources have been strained.

4. Because Green Revolution seeds are being adopted so
   widely, the genetic diversity in seeds is rapidly reducing, and
   local strains are being phased out.

   > ➤ This genetic uniformity places the food supply at an
   > increased vulnerability to diseases and pest infestations.

5. Green Revolution farming often requires more mechanized
   farming techniques that need expensive fuels to power
   farm machines, which increase pollution and fossil fuel
   consumption.

G. Biotechnology

1. *Agricultural biotechnology* is using living organisms to
   produce or change plant or animal products.

2. *Genetic modification* is a form of biotechnology that uses
   scientific, genetic manipulation of crop and animal products
   to improve agricultural productivity and products.

   > ➤ Reorganizing plant and animal DNA and tissue culturing
   > are two examples of genetic modification processes in
   > agricultural biotechnology.

3. Recent innovations in biotechnology have led to plant and
   animal cloning as well as "super-plants" that grow at much
   faster rates, even in nutrient-poor soils, and already have
   pesticides and fertilizers integrated into their DNA.

➤ Scientists have created some crops that are drought-resistant and others that are not susceptible to plant diseases.

➤ Genetically modified animals are manipulated and cloned to produce larger, better agricultural outputs, such as the "super-chicken," which produces more meat at a faster rate.

4. This extension of scientific innovation to all crops and animal products is known as the *Biorevolution*.

 VIII. **Hunger and the Food Supply**

A. Undernutrition and Famine

1. *Undernutrition* is defined as not getting enough calories or nutrients.

2. *Famine* is mass starvation resulting from prolonged undernutrition in a region during a certain period.

B. Solving World Hunger

1. The causes of world hunger exist largely in the distribution of food supplies and people's ability to access food supplies, not in our ability to grow food.

2. While biotechnological research in agriculture promises innovations in humans' ability to further master environmental constraints, it is the social and economic structure inherent in inequality that causes food-security issues, undernutrition, and famine.

3. The solution to ending world hunger is believed to be not just in growing enough food but also in distributing it and empowering people with the *ability* to obtain their needed food and produce *sustainable yields,* or rates of crop production that can be maintained over time.

C. Ester Boserup's Theory

1. Geographer *Ester Boserup* believed subsistence farmers want the most leisure time they can have, so they farm in ways that will allow them to feed their families and maximize free time.

2. In Boserup's theory, she asserts that subsistence farmers will change their approach to farming if the population increases and more food is needed.

3. In this way, Boserup considered the food supply to be dependent on human approaches, thus contrasting with Thomas Malthus's theory of human overpopulation outpacing growth of the food supply.

4. Most evidence shows Boserup's theory is true in a subsistence economy, but not in a technologically-advanced industrialized society.

D. Soil Erosion

1. Due to population pressures, farmers in many regions are trying to grow food at faster rates and often do not allow their soils enough time to recuperate from the last harvest before starting another.

2. Such a practice leads to the negative consequence of *soil erosion*, the loss of the nutrient-rich top layer in soil.

   ➤ Some geographers estimate that nearly 7 percent of the world's rich topsoil is being destroyed each decade.

E. Desertification and Deforestation

1. *Desertification*, another negative consequence related to human overuse of Earth's land, is the loss of habitable land to the expansion of deserts.

   ➤ Though desertification can result from both human and natural causes, humans have contributed to the expansion of the Sahara desert (and other deserts) because of their overly intense use of the land.

2. *Deforestation*, the loss of forested areas, is caused by humans chopping down forest areas at rates so fast that the forested areas cannot regenerate.

➤ Some experts predict that the rainforest centered around the Equator will be completely destroyed in less than a century.

F. Debt-for-Nature Swaps

1. In trying to save precious land resources, governments and organizations have organized *debt-for-nature swaps*, which forgive international debts owed by developing countries in exchange for these countries protecting valuable, natural land resources from human destruction.

Industrialization and Economic Development

I. **Defining Industrialization**

A. Industrialization and the Economy

1. *Industrialization* is the growth of manufacturing activity in an economy or a region.

2. Usually, industrialization is accompanied by a decrease in the number of subsistence farmers in a country or region as they leave the agricultural sector in favor of manufacturing jobs.

3. The *economy* is the system of production, consumption, and distribution in a region.

B. Major Economic Classifications

1. The *primary sector* is the part of the economy in which activities revolve around getting raw materials from the Earth.

   ➤ Farming, fishing, and raw mining are examples of primary economic activities.

   ➤ Industrialized economies have a small proportion of primary sector employment.

2. *Secondary sector* economic activities deal with processing these raw materials (acquired through primary activities) into a finished product of greater value, such as taking raw corn and processing it into baby food.

   ➤ Factories fall into the secondary economic activity category, as factories take raw materials and transform them into finished products.

➤ Manufacturing is a secondary economic activity.

3. *Tertiary sector* economic activities or services are those that move, sell, and trade the products made in primary and secondary activities.

➤ Tertiary economic activities also involve professional and financial *services*, including bank tellers, carpet cleaners, and fast-food workers.

4. *Quaternary sector* economic activity involves information creation and transfer.

➤ Quaternary economic activities assemble, distribute, and process information; they also manage other business operations.

➤ University researchers and investment analysts are examples of quaternary economic activities.

5. *Quinary sector* economic activities exist as a sub-classification of quaternary activities and involve the highest-level of decision making, such as decisions made by a legislature or a presidential cabinet.

➤ High-level, government-targeted research is also included in the quinary sector.

 The Diffusion of Industrialization

A. The History of the Industrial Revolution

1. The *Industrial Revolution* began in England in the 1760s when the industrial geography of Great Britain changed significantly and later diffused to other parts of Western Europe.

2. In this period of rapid socio-economic change, machines replaced human labor and new sources of energy were found. Coal became the leading energy source, fueling Great Britain's textile-focused industrial explosion.

3. The beginnings of assembly-line manufacturing was a defining feature of Great Britain's industrial revolution, later adapted by Henry Ford into what we know today.

   ➤ Although assembly lines existed first on a small scale in people's homes prior to the "revolution," the 1760s saw the growth of large, mechanized factories.

4. Because early factories were powered by coal sources, they tended to clump around coal fields.

   ➤ Northern-central England's coalfields led to the rise of major industrial cities such as Manchester and Liverpool, England. These cities grew due to large rural-urban migration.

   ➤ The emergence of so many factories led to the development of a clear industrial landscape and working-class housing areas.

5. Along with this industrial growth, England's transportation infrastructure improved to allow for shipping supplies into urban factories.

6. Farming also became more mechanized with the infusion of greater technology into the agricultural process.

7. While original factory-like labor was conducted in households through cottage industries, the growth of factories first occurred around water sources, such as rivers and lakes.

   ➤ With the growth of coal-powered manufacturing, factories could move away from the water-sources that formerly supplied energy through steam and water-mill methods.

8. By the 1960s, oil became a dominant source of energy in the world. Although the United States, Russia, and Venezuela had been the chief sources of oil, the surge in oil demand allowed the Middle East to take over the market for oil in the 1960s.

B. Commodification of Labor

1. One result of industrialization was the *commodification of labor*. Factory owners began looking at their human labor as commodities (objects for trade) with price tags per hour, rather than seeing workers as people.

C. The Spread of the Revolution

1. By 1825, the technology of the industrialization in England had spread to North America and Western European countries such as Belgium, Germany, and France.

   ➤ Industrialization thrived in places with rich coal deposits, like Ohio and Pennsylvania in America, Ukraine in Russia, and the Ruhr region in Germany.

2. By the 1920s, the production process in the U.S. automobile factories had broken down into differentiated components, with different groups of people performing different tasks to complete the product, a process known as the *Ford* (or *Fordist*) *production method*.

   ➤ Fordist factories built "out" rather than "up," meaning that they were built on only one story so that the product could be transported throughout the assembly line without problems.

   ➤ The Fordist production method was based on the *division of labor*, where different parts of the assembly process were divided up among different workers and areas of the factory.

III. Explaining and Predicting Where Industries Locate

A. Alfred Weber's Least Cost Theory of Industrial Location

1. Early 20th-century German economist Alfred Weber set out to predict and explain where factories would choose to locate and grow.

2. Just as von Thünen studied the locations of agricultural activities, Alfred Weber studied the locations of industrial activities by setting up a hypothetical state with several assumptions.

3. Weber's model was called *Least Cost Theory* because it predicted where industries would locate based on the places that would be the lowest cost to them.

4. Industries wanting to locate where transportation costs are minimized must consider two issues: the distance of transportation to the market and the weight of the goods being transported.

On a past AP Human Geography exam, over 1/3 of the test takers did poorly on an FRQ that asked about Weber's Least Cost Theory. Many students confused Weber's theory with von Thünen's model of rural land use. Be sure you know the names of models well enough so that you don't confuse them on test day!

B. Assumptions in Weber's Model

1. Transportation cost is determined by the weight of the goods being shipped and the distance they are being shipped.

   ➤ The heavier the good and/or the farther the distance, the more expensive it is to ship.

2. Industries are competitive and aim to minimize their costs and maximize their profits.

3. Markets are in fixed locations.

4. Labor exists only in certain places and is not mobile.

5. Like in the von Thünen model, the physical geography (land quality) and political-cultural landscape are assumed to be uniform across the model's geographic space.

➤ In other words, Weber's model assumes a uniform landscape with equal transportation paths and routes throughout the space (no mountains, lakes or rivers would get in the way).

6. With these assumptions, the location of industry is driven by four factors: transportation, labor, agglomeration, and deglomeration (which we will cover later).

C. Criticism of Weber's Model

1. Weber's theory does not identify the fact that markets and labor are often mobile and that the labor force varies in age, skill sets, gender, language, and other traits.

2. Some transportation costs, unlike in his model, are not directly proportional to distance.

IV. Concepts Related to Weber's Model

A. Weight-Gaining versus Weight-Losing Industries

1. Early factories also had to consider their proximity to the raw materials they needed.

➤ These early factors had *spatially-variable costs*, costs that changed depending on the factory's location.

➤ A factory using heavy or perishable raw materials in its production process might be built as close as possible to its source of raw materials to minimize the cost of transporting the materials into the factory.

2. *Weight-losing processes* are those manufacturing processes that take raw materials and convert them into a product that is lighter than the raw materials that went into making it.

➤ Paper production is an example of a weight-losing production process: many paper mills are located near forests, the source of the heavy wood the factory converts into lighter paper products to be shipped long distances.

➤ When weight-losing industries locate near the raw resource supply, they are said to have a *material-orientation*.

3. *Weight-gaining processes* take raw materials and create a heavier final product.

➤ Beverage bottling is a weight-gaining industry.

➤ Early factories involved in weight-gaining processes were built near the marketplace because the product was heavier to transport in its final form.

➤ When weight-gaining industries locate near the place where the heavier product will be sold, that industry is said to have a *market-orientation*.

B. Footloose Industries

1. *Footloose industries* are not restricted in where they can locate because of transportation costs.

➤ Some industries maintain the same cost of transportation and production regardless of where they choose to locate.

2. These industries have *spatially fixed costs*, costs that remain the same no matter where they choose to locate.

3. These industries often produce lightweight products of extremely high value, like computer chips.

C. Labor Costs and the Substitution Principle

1. The Weber model assumes that the cost of labor is a key factor influencing where industries choose to locate.

2. Included in labor considerations is the availability of *industrial capital*, which consists of machinery and the money to purchase the tools and workers the factory needs.

3. The *substitution principle* applies when an industry will move to a place to access lower labor costs, even though transportation costs might increase as a result.

➤ In the long run, these companies will save more because of the cheaper labor.

D. Agglomeration

1. *Agglomeration* occurs when industries clump together in the same geographic space.

    i. Alfred Marshall first identified the benefits of agglomeration in industrializing England in the late nineteenth century.

2. Factories that are in the same area can share costs associated with resources such as electrical lines, roads, pollution control, etc.

3. *Agglomeration economies* occur when the positive effects of agglomeration (such as lower costs for industries) result in lower prices for consumers.

    i. *Localization economies* are a category of agglomeration economies that occur when many firms in the same industry benefit from clustering close together—for example, these firms get to share skilled labor talents living in the same region.

    ii. *Urbanization economies* are another category of agglomeration economies that occur when large populations in urban areas benefit from clustering together because they get to share infrastructural elements, such as power lines and transport systems.

E. High-Tech Corridor and Technopoles

1. A *high-tech corridor* is a place where technology and computer industries agglomerate.

    ➤ A noteworthy example of a high-tech corridor popped up in California's Silicon Valley, where many tech-related companies located.

2. A *technopole* is another name for a region of high-tech agglomeration, formed by similar high-tech industries seeking to locate in a shared area so that they can benefit from shared resources—like sharing a highly-trained workforce, and utilizing similar support businesses (ancillary services), like computer repair shops and electrical wiring services, etc. (localization benefits).

F. Backwash Effects

1. *Backwash effects* are negative consequences of agglomeration that can occur when other areas suffer out-migration ("brain-drain") of talented people who are moving to a technopole or other "hot spot" of industry agglomeration.

G. Locational Interdependence

1. *Locational interdependence* is the theory that industries choose their locations based on where their competitors are located.

2. Industries want to maximize their dominance of the market, so they are influenced by their competition. Think of seeing so many gas stations at a highway exit. The theory of locational interdependence would assert that these gas stations know that one gas station cannot serve all of the cars needing gas, so agglomerating around the exit allows them a slice of the market share.

H. Deglomeration

1. *Deglomeration* is the "unclumping" of factories because of the negative effects and higher costs associated with industrial overcrowding.

2. Deglomeration often occurs when an agglomerated region becomes too clustered, too crowded, and when such agglomeration negatively affects the industries, such as through pollution, traffic congestion, or strained resources and labor.

V. Development Patterns

A. Development

1. *Development* is the process of improving the material condition of people through the growth and diffusion of technology and knowledge. Every place, regardless of size, exists at some level of development.

B. More Developed vs. Less Developed Countries

1. *More developed countries* (MDCs) are on the wealthier side of the development spectrum.

2. *Less developed countries* (LDCs) are those on the economically poorer side of the spectrum.

3. Both groups of countries have related challenges, with MDCs facing issues such as maintaining economic growth and LDCs trying to improve their economic condition.

4. A country's development level is based not just on how much money it has, but also includes factors related to education and health care development.

C. Gross Domestic Product

1. A country's *gross domestic product (GDP)* is the value of total outputs of goods and services produced in a country, usually over one year.

2. *GPD per capita* is simply the GDP divided by the population.

   ➤ In MDCs, the GDP per capita is usually greater than $20,000, while in LDCs it is often less than $1000.

D. Gross National Product

1. A country's *gross national product (GNP)* includes all goods and services owned and produced by a country overseas.

2. GDP and GNP are often cited as poor measures of development levels because they fail to provide information on factors such as the distribution of wealth, the development of health care and education, and the degree of gender equity in the country.

E. Purchasing Power Parity

1. *Purchasing power parity (PPP)* is a measurement tool for calculating the exchange rates required for each currency to buy an equal amount of goods.

➤ PPP allows economists to make "apple to apple" comparisons among GDP and GNP data.

➤ For example, although the GDP per capita in some sub-Saharan African countries is less than $750, an evaluation of PPP for that income level shows that the buying power in those countries is closer to $4,000 in the United States.

F. Informal Sector

1. A country's (or region's) *informal sector* (or *economy*) includes all business transactions that were not reported to the government.

➤ Unregistered street vendors and day laborers are examples of parts of the informal economy. Other examples of workers performing informal sector economic activities include prostitutes and drug traffickers.

2. A country's GDP does not include transactions in the informal sector.

3. An informal sector of an economy exists for several reasons, including meeting a demand that the formal sector has not fulfilled.

➤ Often, informal sector goods may be so inexpensive (such as street goods) that vendors cannot make enough profit to buy permanent stores and transition into the formal sector.

➤ Also, illegal immigrants risk deportation if they or their employers report their earnings to the government.

G. UN Human Development Index—An Alternative to GDP to Measuring Development

1. *The United Nations Human Development Index (HDI)* is a formula used by the UN to measure a country's development level and compare it to other regions and countries on the rank-ordered list of countries.

2. HDI is based on the ideas that human development is a process of expanding choice for more people, thus pushing countries to improve their education, welfare, health care, and economic systems to include more educational opportunities for more people.

3. The HDI equation uses gross domestic product, life expectancy, educational level attained, and literacy rates to estimate a country's development level and rank it on the list of countries.

4. The highest score a country can get on the HDI is a 1.000, whereas the lowest is 0.000.

H. The Development Gap

1. The *development gap* is the widening difference between development levels in MDCs and LDCs.

2. MDCs are improving in their development levels faster than are LDCs.

➤ In the last decade, the GDP nearly tripled in MDCs but only doubled in LDCs.

➤ The rate of population increase fell by nearly 85 percent in MDCs, but by less than 5 percent in LDCs.

I. The North-South Gap

1. The *north-south gap* refers to the pattern that MDCs are located primarily in the Northern Hemisphere, while LDCs are mainly in the Southern Hemisphere.

VI. Dependency Theory and the Development Gap

A. Defining the Dependency Theory

1. *Dependency theory* argues that LDCs are locked into a cycle of underdevelopment by the global economic system that supports an unequal structure.

2. The dependency theory argues that the political and economic relations among countries limit the ability of LDCs to modernize and develop because the MDCs are dependent upon LDCs to remain at the top of the world economy.

➤ In turn, LDCs remain dependent on MDCs for economic and financial support.

➤ According to the dependency theory, many countries are poor today because of their colonization by Europeans that extracted valuable resources from colonies but did not develop lasting infrastructures that would benefit colonized people after the Europeans left.

3. Dependency theory views the world's countries as existing in a system of interlocking parts. That is, each country's actions impact other countries.

B. Core-Periphery Model

1. The *core-periphery model* states that the world's countries are divided into three groups:

   i. The *core* consists of industrialized countries with the highest per-capita incomes and standard of living.

   ➤ The United States, Canada, Australia, New Zealand, Japan, and western Europe are considered core countries.

   ii. The *semi-periphery* consists of countries that are newly industrialized and have not yet caught up to core countries in level of development, often having vast inequalities in standards of living among their peoples.

   ➤ Countries like Brazil, India, and China exist in the semi-periphery.

   iii. The *periphery* consists of LDCs with low levels of industrialization, infrastructure, per capita income, and standards of living.

   ➤ Most African countries (except South Africa), and parts of Asia and South America are considered in the periphery.

C. Wallerstein's World Systems Analysis

1. *Immanuel Wallerstein's world systems analysis* looks at the world as a capitalistic system of interlocking states connected through economic and political competition.

2. Wallerstein's world systems analysis is linked to the core-periphery model because Wallerstein's theory asserts that the unequal positions of countries grew out of early exploration and colonization that began to create a network, or system, of interrelated economies in the world.

3. Wallerstein argued that colonization by western European countries led to economic and political interactions among different regions (or systems) in the world and the inequalities that resulted from domination and exploitation by core countries of the semi-peripheral and peripheral regions.

4. Wallerstein theorized that the global core, semi-periphery, and periphery grew out of the competitive interactions among different countries.

 VII. **Rostow Modernization Model**

A. Overview of the Model

1. Walt Rostow set out in the 1950s to explain and predict countries' patterns of economic development.

2. Rostow's model consists of five stages through which all countries move as they improve their economic development.

3. MDCs exist in stages 4 and 5, whereas LDCs are in stages 1 through 3.

4. According to Rostow, once a country starts investing in capital (for example in building factories), it will begin to develop.

B. Walt Rostow's Modernization Model Assumes that all Countries Follow a Similar, Five-Stage Process of Development.

1. *Stage One—Traditional Society:* Economic activity is mainly subsistence farming with little investment in innovation.

2. *Stage Two—Preconditions for Takeoff:* As a region begins to develop, a small group of people initiates innovative "takeoff" economic activities that pave the way for economic development.

   ➤ South Korea's development-level improved after its country invested in the high-tech computer "takeoff" industry that led to significant economic improvement.

3. *Stage Three—Takeoff:* The small number of new industries that begin to emerge in Stage Two begin to show rapid economic growth. In this stage, industrialization increases and subsistence farming decreases in the regions where the "takeoff" industries exist.

4. *Stage Four—Drive to Maturity:* At this stage, more advanced technology and development begins to spread to a wider region and other industries (not just the "takeoff") begin to experience rapid growth and workers become more skilled and educated.

5. *Stage Five—High Mass Consumption:* The economy shifts from the dominance of secondary factory jobs to the dominance of service-oriented jobs that require higher levels of education. In this stage, Rostow predicted that a country experiencing higher economic development would lead to higher levels of consumption.

C. Criticisms of Rostow's Model

1. Some geographers do not think the Rostow model can be used to explain and predict all countries' economic development because Rostow based his projections on the pattern of western European and Anglo-American countries.

2. Rostow's model does not consider structural issues that might limit a country's ability to develop, such as post-colonial dependency.

3. Rostow's model also considers each country an independent agent, rather than one piece of an interlocking system of countries.

4. Stage five assumes that higher economic productivity leads to high mass consumption of goods and services. Some geographers argue that a highly productive economy might not lead to such consumption patterns, as Rostow predicts, but could lead to higher levels of social welfare activities or more sustainable activities.

VIII. Approaches to Improving Economic Development

A. Self-Sufficiency Approach

1. To reduce the development gap between rich and poor countries, less developed countries must build their economies more rapidly.

2. The *self-sufficiency approach* pushes under-developed countries to provide for their own people, independent of foreign economies.

3. According to this approach, a country should spread its investments and development equally across all sectors of its economy and regions.

4. Rural areas must develop along with urban areas, and poverty must be reduced across the entire country.

5. The self-sufficiency approach favors a closed economic state, in which imports are limited and heavily taxed so that local businesses can flourish without having to compete with foreign companies.

6. Critics argue that self-sufficiency and closed economies stifle competition, which leads to higher efficiency and innovation.

B. International Trade (Export-Oriented) Approach

1. The *international trade approach* pushes under-developed countries to identify what it can offer the world and then direct investment towards building on that industry.

2. Eventually, a country will develop an advantage over the rest of the world in producing that good or service.

3. A country has a *comparative advantage* when it is better at producing a particular good or offering some service than another country.

   ➤ The place with a comparative advantage can fill the market's need for a good or service at a lower production cost than other places can.

   ➤ Japan invested much money and power in developing a comparative advantage in high-tech products and could produce computer parts more efficiently than other countries could.

   ➤ Once Japan developed a comparative advantage in high-tech products, it could export these products to other countries in exchange for goods that Japan needed to survive and thrive.

C. Structural Adjustments

1. The movement to improve socioeconomic development in LDCs involves supranational organizations like the World Bank and the International Monetary Fund (IMF) that regulate international trade and supply money to developing regions in the form of loans.

2. *Structural adjustments* are requirements attached to a loan from a lending agency like the IMF that force the country receiving the loan to make economic changes in order to use the loan.

3. Often structural adjustments force loan-receiving countries to increase *privatization*, the selling of publicly-operated industries to market-driven corporations.

➤ Privatization can cause hardships for many families that once depended on government owned or operated resources being sold off to profit-driven corporations.

➤ Many African countries underwent structural adjustments requiring them to sell off water systems to private companies that began charging people for the water that was once free when operated by the government.

➤ Advocates of structural adjustment programs argue that long-term economic benefits will outweigh the short-term side effects of difficult economic adjustments.

D. Non-Governmental Organizations

1. *Non-governmental organizations (NGOs)* are organizations run by charities and private organizations, rather than a government agency, that provide supplies, resources, and money to local businesses and causes that advance economic and human development.

➤ Doctors Without Borders and Save the Children are examples of NGOs.

IX. Globalization

A. Defining Globalization

1. *Globalization* is the term used to describe the increasing sense of interconnectedness and spatial interaction among governments, cultures, and economies.

2. Originally, globalization was used in reference to the spread of economic activities from a home country to other parts of the world, but its reach has profoundly influenced cultural and political realms, too.

➤ The globalization of a fast-food chain restaurant is essentially the spread of an economic activity but it also carries with it aspects of culture.

B. Multinational Corporations

1. *Multinational corporations (MNCs)* are businesses with headquarters in one country and production facilities in one or more other countries.

   ➤ MNCs are sometimes referred to as *transnational corporations (TNCs)*.

2. MNCs are primary agents of globalization.

3. MNCs are often *conglomerate corporations*, meaning that one massive corporation owns and operates a collection of smaller companies that provide it with specific services in its production process.

   ➤ A conglomerate corporation might own a bottling company and a food-coloring company.

C. Outsourcing

1. *Outsourcing* is the practice of an MNC to relocate a piece (or all) of its manufacturing operations to factories in other countries.

   ➤ A company headquartered in the United States outsources it shoe production process to workers in Malaysia and other less-developed countries.

2. MNCs often outsource to take advantage of lower labor costs, lower tax rates, and cheaper land prices in countries outside of the United States or their home countries.

3. Remember the *substitution principle*: companies might choose to take on higher transportation costs of moving their industrial location farther from their market because they will end up saving money in the long run by hiring less expensive labor.

D. New Industrial Countries

1. *New industrial countries (NICs)* are countries that have recently established an industrialized economy based on manufacturing and global trade.

E. Asian Tigers

1. Whereas MNC headquarters tend to exist in the United States, Canada, Germany, the United Kingdom, France, and Japan, several NICs like Taiwan, South Korea, Hong Kong, and Singapore experienced rapid economic growth in the late 20th century.

2. The *Asian Tigers* of Taiwan, South Korea, Hong Kong, and Singapore followed the growth patterns of post–World War II Japan by developing a comparative advantage for high-tech products.

3. Together with China and Japan, the four Asian Tigers make up the core of the *Pacific Rim economic region*.

F. Foreign Direct Investment and Special Economic Zones

1. *Foreign direct investment* is investment by a MNC in a foreign country's economy.

2. Often, countries wanting to attract foreign direct investment by MNCs establish *special economic zones (SEZs)*, which are regions that offer special tax breaks, eased environmental restrictions, and other incentives to attract foreign business and investment.

   ➤ China's Communist government has designated SEZs within its territory to allow foreign companies to have free-trade rights and to outsource.

3. *Export processing zones* are regions that offer tax breaks and loosened labor restrictions in LDCs to attract export-driven production processes, such as factories producing goods for foreign markets.

   ➤ Often, export processing zones are referred to as *free-trade zones* because duties and tariffs are waived by governments wanting to encourage MNCs to invest in their countries.

G. Maquiladoras

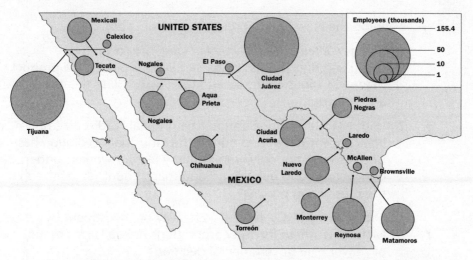

Maquiladora Zones on the Mexico-U.S. Border

1. Mexico established *maquiladora zones*, special economic zones on its northern border with the United States.

2. MNCs can outsource labor to these maquiladoras, taking advantage of labor costs in Mexico that are lower than those required for U.S. workers to manufacture the same products.

3. Additionally, the Mexican government gave tax breaks to U.S. MNCs that located in maquiladora zones, and the products manufactured in maquiladoras could be shipped to U.S. markets tariff free.

4. As part of the *North American Free Trade Agreement (NAFTA)*, the maquiladora program is supposed to be phased out.

X. The New International Division of Labor

A. Defining the New International Division of Labor

1. The *new international division of labor* breaks up the manufacturing process by having various pieces of a product made in various countries and then assembling the pieces in another country.

2. With the rise of globalization, the original Fordist assembly-line concept developed during the Industrial Revolution has been split up not only among many factory workers under one factory roof, but also among many countries involved in the production process.

3. Often, many LDCs depend so heavily on investment by MNCs that these foreign corporations hold a large amount of power over governmental decisions.

B. Free Trade versus Fair Trade

1. *Free trade* is the concept of allowing MNCs to outsource without any regulation except for the basic forces of market capitalism.

   ➤ Critics of free trade argue that free trade only protects the interests of MNCs and does nothing to safeguard workers' rights.

2. *Fair trade* involves oversight of foreign direct investment and outsourcing to ensure that workers throughout the world are guaranteed a living wage for their work.

3. The effects of globalization on the peripheral countries are hotly debated.

   ➤ While some geographers and economists argue that foreign direct investment is helping to generate increased economic development in LDCs, others contend that workers (particularly women) in those countries are being exploited by profit-driven MNCs.

XI. **Globalization and the Environment**

A. Sustainable Development

1. With the diffusion of industrialization and increased economic interaction, geographers wonder if the increased rate of production and development can be maintained while natural resources are being rapidly depleted.

2. *Sustainable development* is a rate of growth and resource-consumption that can be maintained from one generation to another.

   ➤ The UN Commission on Sustainable Development calls for conservation and careful use of resources, focusing on caring for the soil, avoiding overfishing the oceans and rivers, preserving the forests, protecting species from extinction, and reducing air pollution.

B. Ecotourism

1. Because transportation technology has improved so much, humans can travel to places once considered too distant.

2. Many exotic landscapes and "vacationable" areas are being transformed to meet tourists' desires, often at the expense and destruction of local communities and environments.

3. *Ecotourism* comprises tourist operations that aim to do as little harm to the environment as possible.

   ➤ Instead of tearing down a forest to build a theme park, an ecotourist business might build a tourist attraction around hiking through the forest and celebrating its ecological diversity.

C. Greenhouse Effect and Global Warming

1. Geographers are also concerned with the rising average global temperature, caused in part by the spread of industrialization and the related increase in consumption and pollution.

2. The *greenhouse effect* is caused by industrial outputs such as carbon dioxide and methane in the atmosphere that create a vapor that transforms radiation into heat, leading the Earth's temperature to rise.

3. *Global warming theory* argues that the Earth's rise in temperature is causing negative consequences, such as premature melting of the polar ice caps, which could cause a rise in sea levels and an interruption of oceanic patterns.

Test Tip

When taking the AP Human Geography exam, be sure to focus your mind on your own work. Do not pay attention to the other test takers in the room. Many students feel intimidated when people around them seem as if they are finished or working at a different pace. Remember that test booklets often have different orders of questions and students work in different ways. Focus on your own pace and your own work— don't let others throw off your concentration!

Cities and Urban Land Use

I. Urbanization

A. Defining Urbanization

1. *Urbanization* is the growth and diffusion of city landscapes and urban lifestyle.

   ➤ It can be difficult to define and identify a city, since not everyone agrees on the number of people needed to classify a city. Many geographers believe that there is a spectrum or scale of how urban a place is.

2. While most MDCs (more-developed countries) are highly urbanized, the number and percentage of urban dwellers in poorer, less-developed countries has grown massively in recent years.

3. Many city governments in less-developed regions are trying to manage such explosive urbanization. In fact, about 10 million people die each year because of hazardous conditions caused by overcrowding and inadequate infrastructural support in areas experiencing explosive urbanization.

B. Metropolitan Statistical Areas

1. The U.S. Census Bureau uses the term *metropolitan statistical area (MSA)* to identify a geographic unit of area including a central city and all of its immediately interacting counties with commuters and people directly connected to the central city.

   i. An MSA is an urbanized region with a minimum of 50,000 people in it.

ii. Often, the boundaries of MSAs overlap, such as those boundaries of the cities in what is called the "Triangle" in North Carolina. Raleigh, Durham and Chapel Hill all started out as individual cities or towns and have grown into one another, becoming so interrelated that they are now seen as one MSA.

iii. Such a massive, urban "blob" of overlapping, integrating metropolitan areas, whose distinctive boundaries are increasingly becoming difficult to find, was named *"megalopolis"* by geographer Jean Gottmann, who was originally referring to the fusing metropolitan areas of Washington, D.C., and Boston.

2. The U.S. Census Bureau also uses a unit called a *micropolitan statistical area* that is an area of the surrounding counties integrated into a central city with a population of 10,000 to 50,000. Many formerly "rural" areas have been reclassified as "micropolitan" statistical regions.

C. Rate of Urbanization versus Level of Urbanization

1. *Rate of urbanization* is the speed at which the population is becoming urban.

2. *Level of urbanization* is the percentage of people already considered urban.

3. The level of urbanization in the United States is nearly 75 percent, meaning that nearly 75 percent of the U.S. population lives in urban places. However, the rate of urbanization in the United States is much lower than the rate of urbanization in China, which is experiencing a rapid *rate* of urbanization despite its lower overall *level* of urbanization, which is nearly 30 percent.

II. Where Urbanization Began

A. Urban Hearths

1. Geographers analyze where urbanization first developed and why urbanization began in these *urban hearth areas* (places where urbanization first developed).

2. Geographers also analyze the path of urbanization's diffusion from these hearths and the related gaps in urban development among different countries, some of which are nearly 100-percent urban, while others are still largely rural.

3. Several qualities are common among places that were urban hearths: a dependable water supply, a long growing season, domesticated plants and animals, plenty of building materials, and a system of writing records.

B. Agricultural Urban Hearths

1. The earliest cities were born around 3500 BCE and were spawned from agricultural villages.

   i. Earliest hearths of urbanism existed in Mesopotamia, between the Tigris and Euphrates rivers; the Indus River region in modern Pakistan; the Nile Valley in modern Egypt; the Huang He River Valley in modern China; Mexico and Peru.

C. Trade-Based Urban Hearths

1. Some cities grew as established marketplaces, where traders came together to buy and sell goods from across the region.

2. Urbanism spread westward throughout the Mediterranean region because of Phoenician, Greek, and Roman traders, while it spread eastward through overland and caravan trade routes through Persia and Pakistan to India, China, and then Japan.

3. Even at this early stage, specialization began to occur, as certain cities began to focus economic development on the goods over which they had a comparative advantage.

i. Specialization would evolve into the modern, global economic network of specialized cities, each defined largely by its dominant economic specialty, such as Hollywood's specialization in movie-making.

D. Greco-Roman Urban Hearths

1. Greeks and Romans erected cities as centers of political and administrative control over their conquered regions. Such cities often were built in a planned, grid-like pattern.

E. Religious Urban Hearths

1. Other cities grew as centers of religious ceremony, such as urban places in China that were determined to be holy sites and designed in geometric shapes to reflect related, religious beliefs.

III. Pre-Industrial Cities

A. Pre-Industrial Cities

1. *Pre-industrial cities* are those that developed prior to industrialization and shared several characteristics:

    i. The rural settlements surrounding the urban space provided agricultural products and foodstuffs to the urban dwellers, who, in turn, provided different economic functions.

    ii. Pre-industrial cities served as trade centers and gateways to foreign lands and markets.

    iii. After the fall of the Roman Empire by 600 CE, European pre-industrial cities experienced a decline in development.

B. Pre-Industrial Colonial Cities

1. Colonial cities are those that were built and developed by colonizers in conquered lands.

2. With the growth of European imperialism, the Europeans' drive to grab foreign land and resources fueled their construction and creation of cities in their conquered colonies.

3. European colonial cities shared common characteristics such as wide boulevards and prominent, classical architecture.

4. Colonial cities were constructed with the aim of exporting raw resources from the colonial city back to the mother country.

C. The "Urban-Banana" of Pre-Industrial Cities

1. By the beginning of the 1500s, a majority of cities were located in trade-centers that extended from London to Tokyo, a line of cities known as the *urban banana* because of its crescent or banana-like shape that stretched from London to Tokyo.

   i. The focus of urbanization existed in powerful cities, such as London, Paris, Constantinople, Venice, Cairo, Nanking, Hanchow, and Osaka.

2. This "urban banana" pattern of cities resulted from both site and situation factors.

   i. Site factors are the physical and cultural characteristics of a place that help us learn something about the city, factors like arable land, street layout, and building materials.

   ii. Situation factors are those that relate to how a city fits into the larger urban network, such as proximity to major trade routes and other urban places.

D. Internal Economic Structure of Pre-Industrial Cities

1. Internally, pre-industrial cities often had a diverse mix of economic functions in any given space, rather than specific zoning that came with industrialization.

2. Shops, markets, homes, and government offices could typically be found jumbled together in urban space. Yet, economic segregation often existed, with the wealthier elite living closer to the city center.

3. In feudal European cities, guilds led to clumping of certain functions in particular areas of the towns, which suggests the existence of a crude form of zoning, or functional differentiation.

IV. Industrialization and City Structure

A. The Urban-Industrial Revolution

1. In 1800, only 5 percent of the world's population lived in cities; by 1950, 16 percent lived in cities; by 2010, nearly 50.5 percent of the world's population lived in cities.

2. The diffusion of industrialization is largely responsible for urbanizing the world's people, though at unequal levels.

   i. Over 75 percent of the world's population living in more-developed countries live in urban places; only about 40 percent of the population in less-developed countries live in urban places.

B. The European Industrial Revolution

1. The European Industrial Revolution and its related imperialism triggered this diffusion of city growth.

2. Urbanization grew in a snowball process, as the growth of factories and urban jobs provided attractive opportunities to rural people who struggled to make a living by farming.

3. The Industrial Revolution, which started in England and then diffused to other parts of the world, created a steady rural-urban migration pattern.

   ➤ England's population was 24 percent urban in 1800 and 99 percent by 1999.

C. The Second Agricultural Revolution

1. Supporting this pattern of industrial and urban growth was the demographic transition linked to the second agricultural revolution.

2. Because of more efficient and productive agricultural processes developed in the second agricultural revolution, more workers moved to the cities rather than maintain their farming jobs in rural regions.

   i. This urban migration supplied more workers to the growing factories.

   ii. Improved food supplies also supported an increasing population.

D. The Industrial City

   1. By the mid-1700s, formerly great, land-based trade cities were fading away as sea-trade centers such as St. Petersburg and Bombay began to grow rapidly.

   2. By the early 1900s, most of the world's greatest cities were American or European *industrial cities*, like Manchester, Chicago, and Barcelona, which grew during the Industrial Revolution.

      i. The industrial city had a different function from the pre-industrial city: rather than serving mainly as administrative, religious, trade, or gateway cities, the industrial city's primary function was to make and distribute manufactured products.

E. Shock Cities

   1. This pattern of rapid population growth and urban migration led to growing urban spaces that were, in many ways, overwhelmed with the influx of urban in-migrants.

   2. *Shock cities* are urban places experiencing infrastructural challenges related to massive and rapid urbanization.

      i. The challenging social, economic, and cultural changes that accompanied high rates of urbanization associated with the industrial revolution included slums, hazardous pollution levels, deadly fires, the growth of urban prostitution, and the exploitation of children.

> ➤ Manchester, England, was an early example of a shock city. It grew from having less than 80,000 residents in 1750 to nearly 500,000 urban-dwellers just a century later.

    ii. After it developed in Western Europe, industrialization and urbanization spread to North America. The U.S. city of Chicago saw its population grow from 30,000 inhabitants in 1750, to 500,000 by 1830, to over 1.5 million by 1900 and to over 2.5 million by 2010.

F. Strained Infrastructure and Squatter Settlements

1. An important trend in modern urbanization is its diffusion to less developed parts of the world and its uneven spread. Currently, the highest rates of urbanization are occurring in less-developed countries.

2. Urbanization in less-developed countries is often focused on one or two major cities with a high degree of primacy and centrality, rather than being spread evenly throughout the country's landscape.

    i. Such intensely high rates of urbanization in less-developed countries are straining the infrastructural resources of the growing cities.

3. Large migration streams of young adults moving from rural areas to urban areas allow high numbers of opportunity-seekers into already-strained urban places.

4. Unable to find housing, many new migrants build *squatter settlements (barriadas)*—makeshift, unsafe housing constructed from any scraps they find on the land they neither rent nor own.

Urban Systems and Central Place Theory

A. Defining Urban Systems

1. All urban places are part of an interlocking *urban system* of cities that operate within a network of spatial interaction. In other words, urban places interact with each other and are *interdependent,* not independent, and exist in a spider-web of interacting parts.

2. Geographers analyze the spatial distribution of cities and try to determine why the spider-web of cities looks the way it does.

B. Walter Christaller's Central Place Theory

1. As you recall from the earlier chapter on rural land use, geographer Johann von Thünen studied the geographical patterns of *rural* land use in the 1800s.

2. In the 1930s, German geographer Walter Christaller developed the *central place theory* as a means of studying the geographical patterns of urban land use, specifically looking to explain and predict the pattern of urban places across the map.

3. Similar to von Thünen's model, Christaller's ideal model is based on assumptions of a flat land surface, a uniformly distributed rural population, equal transportation methods spread throughout the space, and an evolutionary movement towards the growth of cities.

C. Main Ideas in Christaller's Central Place Theory

1. *Central places* are urban centers that provide services to their surrounding rural people, collectively referred to as the central place's *hinterland.*

2. The *threshold* is the *minimum* number of people needed to fuel a particular function's existence in a central place.

   i. The more unique and special an economic function is the higher its threshold.

    ii. A doughnut shop has a smaller threshold than a hospital because the doughnut shop requires a smaller population as its customer base; the hospital also requires a larger population in order to draw the level of skilled technicians needed to work in the hospital.

3. The *range of a good or service* is the maximum distance a person is willing to travel to obtain that good or service.

    i. The range of a doughnut shop is much smaller than the range of a hospital because a person is willing to travel much farther for needed medical attention than for a doughnut.

4. *Spatial competition* implies that central places compete with each other for customers.

5. With these ideas, Christaller's model illustrated how and why economic functions drive the locational patterns of cities across geographic space. Higher-order central places contain economic functions with high thresholds and high ranges that require large populations to serve groups of lower-order central places existing around them.

    i. Even the lowest-order central places, with very low-threshold, low-range functions (like the doughnut shop) serve a surrounding population, usually a rural settlement.

D. The Hexagonal Spatial Pattern Predicted by Christaller's Central Place Theory

1. Whereas von Thünen's rural land use model resulted in concentric rings of rural land use, Christaller's central place model predicted a hexagonal pattern of urban, central places.

2. Central places vary in their degree of "economic reach," with "higher-order" central places having larger ranges and thresholds than "lower-order" central places that have smaller ranges and thresholds.

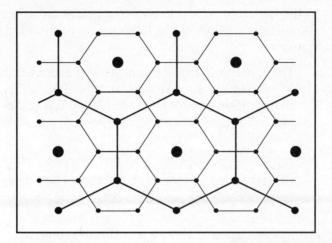

- • Village
- ● Low-Order Central Place
- ⬤ High-Order Central Place

—— Low-Order Market Area Boundary

—— High-Order Market Area Boundary

Hexagonal Market Areas Predicted by Christaller's Central Place Theory

E. Urban Hierarchy

1. Essentially, the central place theory predicts that if a population is evenly distributed, there will be a hierarchy of evenly spread central places to serve that population.

2. Such an *urban hierarchy* is a system of cities consisting of various levels, with few cities at the top level and increasingly more settlements on each lower level.

3. The position of a city within the hierarchy is determined by the types of central place functions it provides.

   i. The higher the position in the hierarchy, the higher the population being served by the central place, and the more variety of central place functions performed in the city. In other words, central places at the top of an urban hierarchy provide functions with the highest ranges and highest thresholds, whereas cities at the lower levels of the urban hierarchy provide lower-range, lower-threshold functions.

4. In the hierarchy, few urban central places are at the top of the hierarchy, while many, lower-order places exist at the bottom.

    i. There are few large cities providing economic functions like Broadway and Wall Street in New York City, and many more, smaller cities, providing gas stations and fast-food restaurants, such as those that exist in smaller places.

    ii. Cities like Chicago sit atop the urban hierarchy in the United States, whereas urban places like Miami and St. Louis occupy the next level of the urban hierarchy.

F. Applying Central Place Theory and Urban Hierarchy: An Example

1. The central place theory provides one piece in the jigsaw of understanding and predicting geographic patterns of urban places.

2. Over the last thirty years, populations in the U.S. South and West have increased and become wealthier overall.

3. With more people and wealth, more services were needed. Several cities stepped up to fill this need—Phoenix, Atlanta, and Dallas moved up on the urban hierarchy as they grew to offer more central place functions to the newly growing populations.

4. As with any hierarchy, as these cities moved up the ladder, other cities moved to fill their places: cities like Tampa, San Antonio, and Charlotte moved up, while some older, manufacturing cities in the Northeast and Midwest began to fall in their rankings within the urban hierarchy.

    i. Remember, the central place theory assumes that people needing a particular service (from buying a doughnut to getting brain surgery) will travel to the *closest* available option to obtain that service. Thus, for example, if a southerner needed to access higher-order central place functions, such as obtaining surgery, he or she no longer needed to travel to Chicago but instead could go to a surgery center in Atlanta.

G. Rank-Size Rule and Centrality

1. There is a relationship between a city's population size and its place on the urban hierarchy within its urban system.

2. A city's ranking in the urban hierarchy can be predicted by the *rank-size rule*, which states that the *n*th largest city's population size in a region is 1/n the size of the region's largest city's population. For example, the 4th largest city in a region is predicted to be 1/4 the size of the region's largest city's population size.

3. While the urban hierarchy in the United States urban system roughly conforms to the rank-size rule prediction, some urban systems have disproportionately large cities, known as *primate cities*.

   i. Cities with such *primacy*, like Buenos Aires, London, Paris, and Rio de Janeiro, are often much, much larger than the second-largest city in the country's urban hierarchy. Buenos Aires, Argentina, is nearly 10 times the size of its second-largest city, Rosario, and thus would have a high degree of *primacy*.

4. Additionally, when a city dominates economic, political, and cultural functions more than you would expect based on its population size, the city also demonstrates a high degree of centrality, or the possession of central place functions.

   i. Managua, Nicaragua, demonstrates urban centrality because its population accounts for only about 30 percent of Nicaragua's total population, but the city controls nearly 40 percent of the country's economy.

VI. World and Megacities

A. World Cities

1. In the interlocking, interacting network of cities throughout the world's urban system, there exist some *world cities*, powerful cities that control a disproportionately high level of the world's economic, political, and cultural activities.

2. Sometimes called *global cities*, world cities have a high degree of centrality in the global urban system.

3. Cities can also be considered world cities because they dominate different areas of global affairs. While Amsterdam is a global financial center, Milan exerts powerful influences over fashion and design.

B. Evolving Distribution of World Cities

1. The group of world cities has shifted with the changing nature of the global urban system. In the 1600s, London, Lisbon, and Amsterdam were world cities in the mercantile economy of that century. By the 1700s, Rome and Paris became world cities. In the 1800s, Berlin, Chicago, New York, and St. Petersburg became world cities with rising industrialization.

2. Today's world cities are less concerned with serving as administrative centers of power over imperialism and trade. Instead, modern world cities are centers of global financial decisions, flows of information, and transnational (or multinational) corporations driving the global economic and political landscape.

3. In addition to being important in the traditional sense as transportation and industrial hubs, a world city's real importance is as a communications hub. In this sense, the physical location of a world city is less important than its ability to be a prominent node in the global communications infrastructure.

C. Pan-Regional Influence

1. World cities have *pan-regional influence*, a reach that extends beyond the city's own region into the other centers of economic control.

   i. New York City is a world city with pan-regional influence because its range extends beyond North America into the other two centers of economic control, Europe/Africa/Middle East and Asia/Oceania.

ii.   New York is home to powerful media outlets, financial institutions, global corporations' headquarters, and political organizations, such as the United Nations, and is a world city because it influences a larger percentage of world affairs than its share of the world's population suggests.

iii. New York City is a world city because its global influence is larger than its share of Earth's population.

D. Megacities

1. Though not considered world cities, *megacities* have a high degree of centrality and primacy, thereby exerting high levels of influence and power in their country's economies.

2. All megacities are large, having over 10 million inhabitants.

3. Beijing, Cairo, Mexico City, and Jakarta are examples of megacities that serve to connect Earth's world cities with the smaller central places in their countries' urban hierarchies.

i.   Jakarta's businesses and political units connect with New York City's services and bring them to Indonesia's people through spatial interactions in the form of trade, transportation, communication, and even migration.

 VII.   **Borchert's Model of Urban Evolution**

A. Borchert Model of Urban Evolution

1. In the 1960s, Samuel Borchert studied cities in the United States and linked historical changes to urban evolution.

2. Borchert's model of urban evolution defined four classifications of cities based on the transportation technology that dominated during the era when the city hit its initial growth spurt and found its comparative advantage in the economy:

i.   Stage 1 cities hit their growth spurt during the "sail-wagon era" of 1790–1830, mostly near ports and waterways for transportation.

ii. In Stage 2, "iron-horse cities" were born and grew around the rivers and canals during the early industrial years of 1830-1870, when the railroad and steam boats were rapidly spreading.

iii. Stage 3 "steel-rail epoch" cities of 1870-1920 hit their spurt during the Industrial Revolution and, because of the steel industry, these industrial cities blossomed, particularly around the Great Lakes.

iv. Stage 4 cities were born around 1920 and were intricately linked to car and air travel, leading to a maze of road networks and the rapid spread of suburbs. Stage 4 saw the growth of new, more influential cities in the U.S. South.

VIII. Comparative Models of North American Cities

A. The Central Business District

1. All of the following models possess a *central business district (CBD)*, or original core of a city's economy, like a nucleus of a cell. However, the degree of influence and geographic location of the CBD varies throughout the different models.

B. Concentric Zone Model

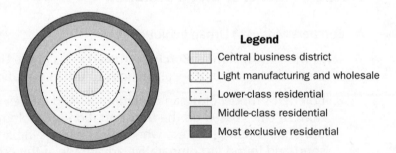

Legend

- Central business district
- Light manufacturing and wholesale
- Lower-class residential
- Middle-class residential
- Most exclusive residential

Concentric Zone Urban Land Use Model

1. Developed in the 1920s by E.W. Burgess, the *concentric zone model* was the first model to explain and predict urban growth.

2. Based on urban growth in Chicago, the concentric zone model is the original foundation upon which the other models of urban growth are built.

3. The model suggests that a city's land use can be viewed from above as a series of concentric rings, like the rings of a tree trunk that has been cut.

    i.   As the city grows and expands, new rings are added and older rings change their function and character. For example, a ring of land use where houses were once built might become a business sector, with the old houses being transformed into offices.

4. The model assumes a process sometimes called *invasion and succession* or *succession migration*, in which new arrivals to cities tend to move first into the inner rings, nearer to the CBD, which then pushes the people and economic activities already present out into farther rings.

5. Because of this constant invasion and succession pattern, often there exists a ring, known as the *zone in transition*, just outside of the CBD that never becomes developed because investors know it will constantly be caught in this shifting urban pattern. Sometimes this zone in transition is called "skid-row."

6. In the concentric zone model, the CBD is the premiere land-use ring nearest the point of maximum accessibility and visibility in the city, a point known as the *peak land value intersection*.

    i.   The highest real estate prices and competition for land is found in this model's CBD.

    ii. Land values decrease moving in all directions away from the CBD, so that the farther out a ring of urban land use, the less expensive the land.

7. The *bid-rent curve* predicts that land prices and population density decline as distance from the CBD increases.

i. A ritzy real estate firm would want to buy a sleek headquarters in the heart of the CBD to show importance in the community and also to have access to the downtown's powerful people and businesses. A factory, however, would be less likely to locate in or near the CBD, because it can purchase more land for less money to build its factory.

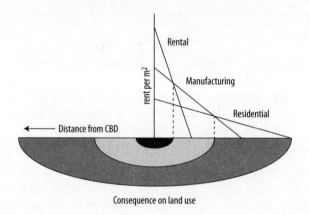

Consequence on land use

Bid-Rent Curve

ii. Bid-rent curves show the variations in rent different users pay for land at different distances from some peak point of accessibility and visibility in the market, often the CBD. Because transportation costs increase as you move away from the market (often the CBD), rents usually decrease as distance increases from the market.

➤ Importantly, different types of land use (commercial retail, industrial, agriculture, housing) generate different bid-rent curves.

➤ Bid-rent curves explain the series of concentric rings of land use found in the concentric zone model.

8. The concentric zone model shows a pattern in which the architectural form and function of buildings match in each concentric ring of urban land use.

    i. The architecture of the houses in a concentric ring occupied by suburban families matches its function to provide families with houses. A suburban-style house is not a likely sight in the heart of Chicago's CBD.

C. The Sector Model

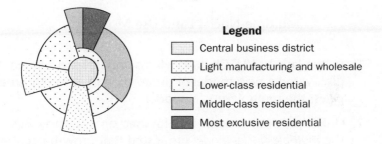

Legend

☐ Central business district

☐ Light manufacturing and wholesale

☐ Lower-class residential

☐ Middle-class residential

☐ Most exclusive residential

Sector Land Use Model

1. In the 1930s, Homer Hoyt discovered a twist on the concentric zone pattern, known as the *sector model.*

2. The sector model grew out of observations that there were urban land-use zones of growth based on transportation routes and linear features like roads, canals, railroads, and major boulevards, not just concentric zones around the CBD.

3. The sector model explained that similar land uses and socioeconomic groups clumped in geometric sectors radiated outward from the city's CBD along particular transportation routes.

    i. Many factories and industrial activities followed rail lines; lower socioeconomic housing followed lines of public transportation; and visitor services sectors were located along major highways.

D. The Multiple-Nuclei Model

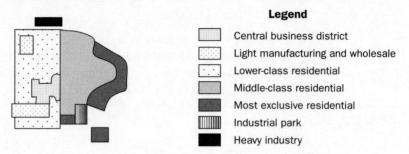

Legend

	Central business district
	Light manufacturing and wholesale
	Lower-class residential
	Middle-class residential
	Most exclusive residential
	Industrial park
	Heavy industry

Multiple-Nuclei Land Use Model

1. By the late 1940s, Chauncy Harris and Edward Ullman discovered a new model of urban growth in North American cities: the multiple-nuclei model.

2. Unlike previous models that focused on a strong CBD, the *multiple-nuclei model* suggested that growth occurred independently around several major focal points, like airports, universities, highway interchanges, and ports.

   i. These focal points may be distant from the "original" CBD and only loosely connected to it, suggesting a reduced dominance of the CBD in urban growth.

3. The multiple-nuclei model recognized that land use zones often popped up at once, in chunks.

   i. Industrial parks, shopping centers, and housing zones could be built in one, giant sweep of construction and be only very loosely connected to the original heart of the city.

4. The model does not suggest that the CBD is necessarily unimportant, but it does show that new areas of intense, urban growth (called nuclei) can grow simultaneously around key nodes of access or industry.

E. The Urban Realms Model

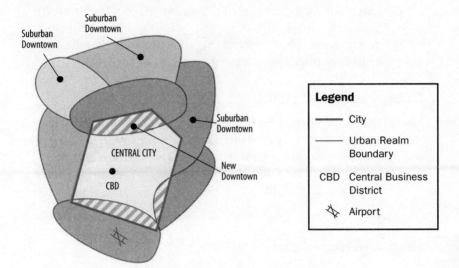

Urban Realms Urban Land Model

1. As the automobile became increasingly prevalent, the *urban realms model* was developed in the 1960s by James Vance to explain suburban regions that were functionally tied to mixed-use, suburban downtowns with relative independence from the CBD.

   i.   Vance developed the model while observing the sprawling growth of the San Francisco Bay area metropolis.

2. This model grew from the increasing independence developed by the "nuclei" within the multiple-nuclei growth pattern. Beyond simply being focal points of urban growth, these nuclei evolved into independently functioning "urban realms."

3. The urban realms model recognized that many people's daily lives and activities occurred within a fixed activity space within a portion, or urban realm, of a larger metro region. In these "urban realms," one could find suburban downtowns, filled with all the amenities needed for living, including businesses, eateries, medical care, etc.

F. Comment on all Models

1. The classic urban systems models can be combined in order to understand a particular city's urban growth pattern. Rings and sectors with a variety of nuclei and realms existing farther from the CBD along a beltway, for example, may encircle a city's CBD.

IX. Latin American Cities

A. Model of Latin American Cities

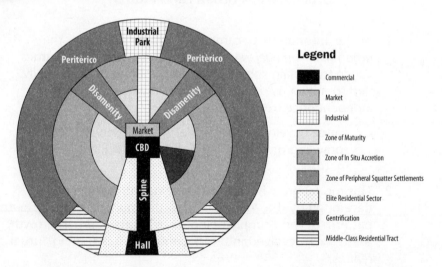

Latin American City Structure Model (Ford-Griffin Model)

1. Larry Ford and Ernest Griffin created a model of the pattern of urban growth in Latin America, particularly regions colonized by Spain.

2. While most medieval cities in Europe were laid out in unplanned jumbles of open-spaces and intertwined streets, the 1400s saw a rebirth in Renaissance, Greco-Roman architecture, and street/urban design, which the Europeans diffused throughout their colonies.

   i. Spain passed a law in 1573 ordering that all of its colonial cities would be built according to Greco-Roman designs, with prominent, rectangular plazas dominated by a Catholic Cathedral and major governmental buildings. These plazas resembled sectors in the North American sector model.

3. Commercial and residential zones encircled the Latin American plaza, similar to the CBD in the North American city.

   i. The CBD was more important in the focus of Latin American cities because suburbanization was not nearly as strong in Latin America.

4. In the Latin American city, wealth typically decreases as one moves outward from the downtown area.

   i. Typically, one can find squatter settlements and abject poverty in rings outside of the CBD in Latin American cities.

5. *Perifericos* are zones of peripheral squatter settlements in Latin American cities. Squatter settlements often grow in Latin American cities because massive numbers of migrants from rural regions move towards urban areas in hopes of new economic activities.

6. A *zone of in situ accretion* is a region transitioning towards maturity and development that is a mix of middle-income and lower-income families and make-shift housing.

7. A *zone of maturity* includes services and infrastructural development.

On a previous AP exam, students were asked to analyze megacities in the periphery. However, many students wrote about large cities in core regions (Europe, Japan, and North America)—not in the periphery. Moreover, many students erroneously wrote about slums, rather than about squatter settlements. Also, many students failed to link the development of squatter settlements in the periphery to rural-urban migration patterns associated with the periphery, as rural workers migrate into cities to earn work. Be very careful to address the specific parts of the question—precisely matching key words used in the question to your response (such as using squatter settlements in your answer, rather than slums).

X. Related Trends

A. Counterurbanization and Exurbs

1. *Counterurbanization* is the increase in rural populations that result from the out-migration of city residents from their city and suburban homes in search of non-urban lifestyles.

2. In the 1950s, geographers saw the growth of *exurbs* (extra-urban areas), or rings of wealthier rural communities that grew just outside of the suburbs and were hotbeds of continued urban growth and development.

   i. Early inhabitants of *exurbs* commuted via parkways systems and commuter rails. Now, many residents of rural areas can work from their homes and send work into distant, city-based headquarters.

3. *Telecommuting* is a modern form of commuting that involves only commuting of information, not the worker, through the use of the telephone and Internet technology.

B. Urban Sprawl

1. Urban sprawl is the diffusion of urban land use and lifestyle into formerly non-urban, often agricultural lands.

2. Urban sprawl has led to the growth of what Joel Garreau called *edge cities,* self-sufficient, urban villages that often develop at highway exits and are part of a larger, metropolitan complex.

> ➤ Cool Springs, Tennessee, is considered by many to be an edge city because it is developed along a highway exit within the metropolitan complex of Franklin, Tennessee. But Cool Springs contains its own neighborhoods, schools, chain restaurants, movie-theatres, business-district, and health resources, among other amenities that make it self-sufficient.

3. Suburbs and edge cities often fight for independence from the metropolitan government so that their inhabitants can have their own mini-governments and tax bases.

   i. Central cities often find themselves surrounded and "strangled" by independently governed suburbs, leaving inner-cities with a limited tax base.

   ii. If the inner-city is predominantly occupied by a lower socio-economic (poorer) tax base, then the amount of taxes the inner-city can collect for its schools and infrastructure is limited.

   iii. St. Louis, Missouri, had nearly 1 million residents in 1950, but by 2010, the city-proper had only 320,000 residents because most people had fled to the independently-governed suburbs surrounding the city.

C. Uneven Development

   1. *Uneven development* refers to urban development that is not spread equally among a city's areas, leaving some areas richly developed and others continually poor and decrepit.

   2. Uneven development is often caused by *cumulative causation,* when money flows to areas of greatest profit, places where development has already been focused, rather than to places of greatest need. Often, opulent skyscrapers and multimillion-dollar malls exist only minutes from some of the poorest, most underdeveloped regions.

D. Ghettoization

1. *Gheottoization* refers to the growth of areas of concentrated poverty.

   i. Urban ghettos were originally comprised of mostly immigrants, such as newly-arrived Irish, Italian, and German people, but even larger African American, Hispanic, and Asian ghettos have grown since the 1950s.

2. Real estate developers and banks contributed to the growth of urban ghettos and sometimes profited from ghettoization, particularly in three ways:

   i. *Blockbusting*—when real estate agents and developers used racism to "bust up" a block by bringing in a minority family into a predominantly white neighborhood and then profiting from all of the real estate turnover that followed.

   ii. *Racial steering*—when real estate agents would intentionally or unintentionally steer people to buy a home in a neighborhood based on their race, which contributed to racially segregated housing patterns.

   iii. *Redlining*—when banks would refuse to give loans to certain minority-occupied neighborhoods that were "redlined," a practice which further entrenched these spaces in urban poverty.

E. Gentrification

1. *Gentrification* is a process wherein older, urban zones are "rediscovered and renovated" by people who move back into the inner-city from the suburban fringes.

2. Gentrification often brings money into inner-urban areas thought to be underdeveloped and poorer.

3. Many people see gentrification as a great solution to recharging a city's inner-core that was suffering due to *suburbanization*, the growth of suburb neighborhoods and commuter families, and the continued flight of wealthier classes out of the inner city.

4. Critics of gentrification see it as only increasing uneven development: they think gentrification is pushing lower-income families from their homes in order to build buildings that only the rich can afford.

    i.   New businesses do come to the region to cater to these rich "gentrifiers," but the people who were originally living in the neighborhood often can't afford to patronize these new businesses or buy into the gentrified housing complexes.

    ii. In this sense, critics claim that gentrification does not help reduce poverty and uneven development, but actually pushes the urban poor from their neighborhoods and divides the urban landscape into ghettos and highly priced, gentrified districts.

F. Containing Urban Sprawl

1. European cities like London, England, have worked to limit urban development to a particular area by installing a green belt, a boundary that forces all urban development to occur within the city's urban core.

    i.   North American cities have a difficult time setting such boundaries because they can attract investors who want to develop these lands and grow the city at the expense of rural lands.

       ➤ Portland, Oregon, is one city that has effectively instituted a boundary to contain urban sprawl. Developers must focus on the land within the established boundary, forcing revitalization of the inner-city and not outward growth. However, while Portland's boundary works to contain urban sprawl, real estate prices and the cost of living increase substantially.

G. Neo-Urbanism

1. *Neo-urbanism* is a movement to bring together trends in healthy living, sustainable growth, and urban development.

2. One neo-urban trend includes constructing *planned communities,* neighborhoods with master-planned housing designs, walkable pathways, recreational facilities, and security features.

    i. One planned community in Memphis includes a small grocery store and ice-cream shop, pedestrian-friendly walkways, a Starbucks, and a golf-cart for each family in the neighborhood.

    ii. Health experts are encouraging North American developers to build in pedestrian walkways to reduce cardiovascular/heart disease, which is increasingly in America partly because of Americans' reliance on automobile travel, rather than walking.

3. Many recent, neo-urban designs include *festival settings*, or large recreational areas for communities, such as waterfront parks along rivers. Boston's Faneuil Hall is an example of a festival marketplace with facilities for food, entertainment, art, etc.

XI. Functional Character of Cities

A. Basic versus Non-Basic Jobs

1. The *basic employment sector* brings money into an urban place and gives the city its primary function.

> Flint, Michigan, was dominated by its basic employment sector of automobile manufacturing. The cars made in Flint's basic employment sector were exported to other places, which, in turn, sent money into Flint's economy for the cars.

> Chapel Hill, North Carolina, is a small city whose basic employment sector is dominated by the existence of the University of North Carolina at Chapel Hill, a basic employment function that exports information and knowledge in exchange for bringing money into Chapel Hill.

2. The *non-basic employment sector* in a city comprises jobs that shift money within the city, not outside of the city as basic jobs do.

➤ Teachers, janitors, fire departments, dry cleaners, street cleaners, and air-conditioner repair companies are all examples of non-basic employment. The non-basic sector is largely responsible for maintaining a city's infrastructure.

3. Usually, the larger a city is, the higher the percentage of non-basic employment jobs because these larger cities often have more infrastructural needs—window washers, dry cleaners, parking lot attendants, subway technicians, etc.

➤ In a smaller city, gas stations and restaurants may be part of its basic-employment sector because residents from nearby rural regions may come into the small town to purchase these services, thereby bringing money into the town from outside.

4. Since most cities have the same types of non-basic jobs, the basic employment sector defines a city and gives it more of its unique sense of place and presence in the economy.

➤ Steel-mill towns, warehouse port facilities, oil refineries, country-music towns, and film industry hotspots are all examples of basic-sector employment types that heavily influence a city's sense of identity.

B. The Multiplier Effect

1. Cities often try to build their economies around the basic sector, which bring in money to the city from outside.

➤ A car factory will bring money in as those cars are produced and sold to people outside of the city.

2. The addition of one more basic job tends to give rise to more jobs, including non-basic jobs, a pattern called the *multiplier effect.*

    i.   The addition of assembly-line jobs in an automobile factory, which are basic jobs producing a good for export and interaction with other places, creates the need for janitors, air-conditioning repair people, electricians, and building inspectors, among other non-basic jobs.

C. The Functional Nature of the Post-Industrial North American City

1. North America's basic employment sectors were once dominated by manufacturing and industrial activities.

2. The nature of America's basic sector of employment is moving away from industrial jobs and towards professional and financial services.

3. *Post-industrial city* economies are focused more on display and consumption rather than on industrial production.

> Old factories are being converted into shopping malls; former waterfront industrial ports are being turned into parks for recreation; old warehouses are being renovated into art galleries.

4. Post-industrial architecture is often characterized by *post-modernism*, a style that emphasizes diversity and free form rather than uniformity and symmetry that characterized the classical Greco-Roman roots of Renaissance and Enlightenment-era buildings.

5. The older, industrial core cities of the United States, like Chicago and New York City, are becoming *deindustrialized,* as their factory-based economies are transitioning to economies dominated by the service sector.

    i.   Such cities have experienced "boom and bust" cycles, in which their service sectors boomed while their manufacturing sectors suffered.

    ii. Other cities, like Austin, Texas, never had a manufacturing base, so the service sectors have boomed without any related industrial bust.

PART III

TEST-TAKING
Strategies

Strategies for Success
with Multiple-Choice Questions

A. Understanding Types of Multiple-Choice Questions

1. If you take the time to review released exams, you'll see that the AP Human Geography exam often uses different types of multiple-choice questions.

2. The following are some broad categories and examples of AP Human Geography multiple-choice questions similar to those seen on released exams:

   (A) *Questions that directly test your knowledge of a key concept.*

   For example:

   Subsistence agriculture

   (A) only includes the herding of animals

   (B) is aimed at producing surplus crops for sale in the market

   (C) is becoming increasingly dominant in the world

   (D) is characterized by production of food for consumption by the farmers and their families

   (E) is most practiced in South America

   The correct answer is (D) since subsistence agriculture is most often practiced in under-developed regions where people can only farm enough food to feed themselves and their families.

   This sample question tests knowledge of the key concept of subsistence agriculture. Chapters in this book will help you acquire knowledge of key concepts needed to answer questions like this.

(B) *Questions that ask you to apply your knowledge of a key concept.*

For example:

Which of the following is the best example of a non-basic employment sector function?

    (A) An assembly-line worker in a car factory

    (B) A video game software engineer

    (C) An international public relations agent

    (D) A university medical researcher

    (E) A police officer

The correct answer is (E), since non-basic sector jobs cause a shift in money within a city, whereas the other jobs create an exchange of money between the city and another place.

If you notice, this question asks you to apply your knowledge of this key concept to examples and choose the best match between non-basic functions and the examples provided. Sometimes, these types of questions will ask you to use a map, table, graph, or image to answer the question.

(C) *Questions that test your knowledge of a specific geographic issue or example.*

For example:

By 2050, which country is projected to have the highest population in the world?

    (A) China

    (B) Indonesia

    (C) Russia

    (D) India

    (E) United States

The correct answer is (D), since India's population growth rate is exceeding China's.

Notice that this type of question is probing your knowledge of this specific demographic trend. While many of these questions seem highly specific, your knowledge of key concepts can often guide you to eliminate options and select from the remaining choices.

B. Ten Strategies for Success on the Multiple-Choice Questions

1. *Underline key words in the question.* Underline all the key terms, concepts, or places. This will help you focus on the key issues in the question.

   For example, if the question asks you,

   > "Which place has the highest percentage of urban residents?"

   Mark it up as follows:

   > "Which place has the <u>highest percentage</u> of <u>urban residents</u>?"

2. *Circle key command words* in a question, such as EXCEPT, ALL, NOT, or BEST. Students often miss questions that use negative logic, such as "All of the following EXCEPT," because they get confused. Be sure you focus your mind on the logic of the question.

3. *Use the process of elimination.* Success is as much about finding the correct answer as it is about getting rid of the wrong answers!

   One of the most powerful strategies is to cross out as many of the wrong answer choices as possible. Many students greatly improve their scores by using this strategy and then selecting their "best educated guess" after ruling out one or two choices that are clearly wrong.

4. *Answer every multiple-choice question.* There is no longer a "guessing penalty," on AP exams, so it is to your advantage to answer *every* multiple-choice question.

5. *Multiple-choice questions are equally weighted.* Since every multiple-choice question is equally weighted, no question counts for more points than another. Therefore, if you are stumped on a question, do not waste too much time on it—but be sure to answer it. Guess—remember there's no guessing penalty!

6. *Fill in your answer sheet as you go.* Remember, you only have 60 minutes to answer 75 questions, which means you have less than one minute to answer a question. It is best to fill in your bubble sheet for each question as you go. Do NOT wait until the end to go back and fill-in the bubbles for all of the questions. If you run out of time and haven't completed filling in your answers on the bubble sheet, you could ruin your score.

7. *Pay attention to your bubble sheet.* Make sure that you have entered your answers correctly on the bubble sheet. As you fill in the bubble sheet, be sure you're filling in the bubble for question 4 when you're working on question 4. If you lose your place and put the answer for question 4 in the bubble for question 5, it will throw off your entire answer sheet and thus your score! Some teachers recommend that, as you work through the multiple-choice section, you write your answers next to the multiple-choice question so that you can transfer your answers accurately from the multiple-choice booklet onto the bubble form and check your bubble sheet easily for a match. If you choose to do this, that's fine, but <u>be aware of your time</u>. You don't want to run out of time while transferring your answers.

8. *Look carefully* at any image, graph, chart, or map provided with a multiple-choice question. Feel free to annotate or draw on these items to help you focus and make sense of them.

9. *Read the question and think of your answer* before you read the answer choices given. This can help your brain select the best choice, rather than falling into distracting traps presented by the wrong answer choices.

10. *Half equals three.* Remember that, based on previous exam scores, you'll need to answer about half of the multiple-

choice questions correctly in order to earn a 3! This, of course, also depends on your FRQ performance . . . so let's move on to strategies for the FRQs. . . .

Strategies for Success
with the Free-Response Questions

A. Understanding the Free-Response Questions

   1. Each FRQ will be testing you on a key concept or group of concepts from the core curriculum. You will be required to answer three FRQs in 75 minutes.

     ➤ According to the College Board, the FRQ section usually includes

        • one question that tests a specific geographic concept and how it applies to a real-world situation;

        • one question that tests how you synthesize your knowledge of Human Geography across the course's topic;

        • one question that tests the depth of your knowledge of a geographic topic and how you can apply this across geographic contexts.

   2. Most FRQs will have multiple-part questions. In the past, FRQs have asked students to answer questions similar to this example (note that the following example would be considered one FRQ):

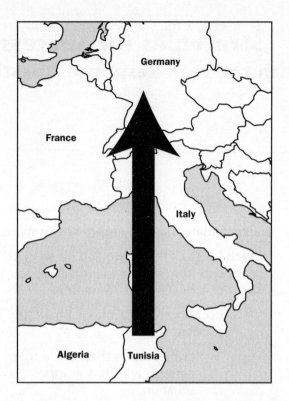

a. Define net in-migration and describe the stream identified in the map above.

b. Define push and pull factors in migration. Give an example of and explain one push and one pull factor that a migrant in the stream shown in the above map may have experienced.

c. Relate the immigration pattern noted on the map to Germany's negative rate of natural increase.

Notice that in the example above, the question prompts you to:

i.   Define key concepts (net in migration, push/pull factors)

ii. Apply key concepts to maps and a relevant example (applying the concepts to the map depicting a migration stream from North Africa into Germany)

    iii. Interrelate key concepts (immigration and rate of natural increase)

B. Important Tips for Success on Free-Response Questions

  1. *Distribute your time wisely*

- Since you only have 75 minutes to answer three FRQs, you should spend approximately 25 minutes on each FRQ.

- You must answer all three questions and all of the multiple parts of each question.

- Some questions may be very straightforward and will not require much time at all. Don't feel as if you need to spend 25 minutes on every question in order to get it right. If you know it, answer it thoroughly, and move on.

- The best way to approach this section is to spend a few minutes previewing all of the questions to make yourself aware of all of the FRQs.

- Begin by outlining your response to your first FRQ or "pre-writing" your initial thoughts for three to five minutes.

- After "pre-writing," spend about 20 minutes on the question formulating your official response in the answer booklet.

- The proctor will probably not warn you until the very end of the 75 minutes, so it will be your responsibility to pace yourself in order to answer each of the three FRQs in the allotted time.

  2. *Bring multiple pens*

- You will need a pen for this section, so bring three of your favorite black- or blue-ink pens (no markers or jelly pens).

- Handwriting is important. If something is illegible—if the AP reader can't read your response—it does not count, even if it is a correct response.

3. *Formatting logistics*

- Be sure that you write the number of the FRQ that you are answering at the top of <u>each</u> of the answer-booklet pages.

- It is a good idea to start each of your answers to the FRQs on a new page in the answer booklet. You've got the whole booklet to use—don't cram your answers onto one page.

4. *FRQs are not essays!*

- Many AP exams require formal essays that involve developing a strong thesis statement and then proving your thesis in well written, supporting paragraphs and ending your essay with a conclusion. AP Human Geo is different: a formal essay is *not* required for this section. (Hooray!) Instead, think of the FRQs as short-answer questions.

- Get right to the point. Don't bother with a thesis paragraph or a conclusion. You get no points for either. Jump right into your response. There's no need to restate the question or start with a thesis statement. *AP readers are only looking for content,* and will not be judging the quality of your writing.

- Official AP exam instructions given in previous years recommend that you label and number each part of your response in the margins of your answer booklet to keep your reader aware of where you are in your response to the FRQ. For example, when you are answering FRQ 1, part A, you might want to label your response in the margin "1A." Then, "1B," and so forth.

- Keep in mind that the easier it is for the AP reader to identify the main points of the question, the easier is it for them to award points to your response. Make it as easy as possible for the AP reader to navigate your response.

5. *Formulate a logical response*

- While a formal essay with a thesis is not required (and not really wanted), simply listing facts is *not* enough.

You need to write in complete sentences with coherent, supported thoughts.

- Support your responses with accurate geographic examples whenever possible.

- If the FRQ asks for examples from a particular region, be certain you use examples from that region and link your examples to the question's prompt.

6. *Review your regions*

- AP readers have commented that students often confuse geographic regions. Therefore, while studying for the exam, take time to review geographic regions: East Asia, Southwest Asia, Western Europe, Eastern Europe, North America, etc.

- While you familiarize yourself with each region, look for examples and situations that you could use in your responses.

C. Scoring the FRQs

- Each of your FRQ responses will be scored by a different reader who is either a college professor or an AP Human Geography teacher. The scoring will be done at an AP-grading convention held during the summer.

- Each FRQ response is graded separately from the others.

- Every AP reader uses a scoring rubric that spells out *exactly* how to give points while grading each FRQ. Therefore, AP readers don't have much flexibility in scoring your response: they have to follow the rubric created by the AP program.

- Remember AP readers *award* points—they don't take points off. You must answer each specific part of each question. You will not be awarded points for any part that you skip. It's that simple. Even well written responses that show some understanding of the FRQ may still earn no points if the response does not include information directly related to the answers the AP readers are looking for based on the rubric they need to follow.

- The three FRQs are weighted equally, so each FRQ is important to your score.

D. How to Score Well on the FRQs

- *Answer the question being asked.* Carefully study the language used in the question. Circle the key words. If it asks you to "define" a term, write a definition. If it asks you to "evaluate," analyze all the parts of the issue. Be direct, don't restate what you are defining—define it and move on.

- *Answer all parts of the question.* If the question asks you to define a term and then give an example, be sure you address both parts of that multi-part question.

- *Be careful if the FRQ calls for a specific type of example.* The question might ask you for an example from a particular time period in history or for a particular region. The FRQ may ask you to give an example of a *country* or it may call for you to cite a *region*, so be careful to use an appropriate example. Don't use an example that doesn't fit. Choose your example carefully and integrate it into your response.

- *Be geographically analytical in your response.* Avoid injecting personal opinions and side comments that distract from your response. Try to draw together appropriate relationships from across different parts of the course. For example, if the FRQ asks you to discuss how globalization is threatening linguistic diversity, you might include treatment of time-space compression and the friction of distance. You might address assimilation, cultural diffusion, or other related concepts. The more you can support your response with substantive geographic examples, the better your response will be scored.

  However, you should not write in random and unrelated ideas just to impress the reader with your geographic vocabulary! Instead, only integrate concepts directly related to the FRQ's focus. Again, the object is to get right to the point and to support your point. There's no need for flowery language or Shakespearean prose.

- *If there is a "stimulus" in the FRQ, such as a chart, map, or graph, be sure that you use and reference it in your response.*

Use specifics from the "stimulus" in formulating your response to the FRQ. It's there for a reason—so use it! Take some time to analyze what the item shows you and how it relates to the FRQ. Feel free to draw on it and mark it up! You don't get points for marking up the question. AP readers only grade the written content in the response booklets.

E. Commonly Asked Questions

Here are some commonly asked questions about the FRQ section:

- **Can I include a diagram or sketch in my FRQ?**

  Yes, you can include a diagram or sketch in your FRQ. However, it is highly recommended that you do not include this as the only piece in your response. If you choose to use a diagram or sketch, link it to your overall response and be sure to describe what it means and how it relates to your response. A diagram shows AP readers that you know what you're talking about, but it is not a sufficient answer on its own.

- **What if I have no idea how to respond to the question?**

  This could happen and the most important thing for you to do is to not panic. More than likely, you can offer some geographic analysis of the issue, even if you are truly stumped. Start writing something related to the course and an issue you think might be tied to the FRQ.

  For example, in a past administration of the exam, some students were stumped by an FRQ calling for an analysis of the distribution of chicken farming in the U.S. Several stumped students started writing about agricultural changes in the U.S., the movement towards agribusiness, and the decline of family-owned farms in the U.S. They were successful because they offered somewhat of a related idea.

  Do *not* leave an FRQ blank. Many well-prepared students find that one of the FRQs is their "challenge FRQ," meaning the one that really gave them a run for their money. If you don't know the answer right away, go with your gut and keep it simple. Don't panic and try to make it sound complicated to cover your tracks. Be simple, direct, and stay in your comfort range and you'll probably be pleasantly surprised with your score.

Note that if you write material that is graphic or can potentially be taken as disturbing or threatening, AP will likely respond and contact your school. Pictures of guns and violence are taken seriously and could lead to real consequences. Know that you will be responsible for what you say and the consequences could be immediate.

- **How long should my FRQ response be?**

There is no right or wrong length for an FRQ response. Long, unfocused responses can confuse and distract the AP reader. If your response fully answers the FRQ, then it is the right length. Be sure you do not spend too much time on one FRQ and lose time to address the remaining FRQs adequately.

- **Will I have enough time to write my answers?**

The AP test is designed not to push you on time constraints, so students generally have just enough time to write their responses. Remember, though, that it is your responsibility to keep an eye on the time and your progress.

- **Do I have to know names of geographers?**

Yes, you should know the names of geographers associated with the major geographic models they invented or major concepts they are credited with studying. On a past exam, students were asked about the "Burgess model," which confused students who did not know that Burgess was the name of the geographer who invented the concentric zone model.

- **How much do I need to know about the world map?**

You need to know the major regions of the world and some key issues going on in these regions. As you review for the exam, note specific examples or concepts tied to particular regions in the world, such as demographic trends or places where religions started or diffused. A recent exam question asked students to look at a map of Europe and a map of the Middle East and name examples of states, nations, and nation-states.

You might want to find an online world map review game to practice identifying countries and regions in the world. There are many great, free map practice sites on the Internet. As you practice with them, think about the human patterns and issues associated with the different regions and countries you are identifying.

You also need to remember that Africa, Europe, and Asia are continents, *not* countries! Also, for purposes of this exam, do not refer to the United States just as "America." Always refer to it as the "United States," though you certainly can state that it is in North America, if necessary.

Test Tip

Be sure to check out the official AP Human Geography webpage on the College Board's website. There you'll find released FRQs, scoring rubrics, and sample student responses for every year that the AP Human Geography exam has been administered. Many students who are successful on the AP exam use these critical resources as practice questions and to see how the FRQs are scored. You should practice these questions under timed conditions to prepare yourself for the actual exam.

Notes